SEA
POOLS

SEA POOLS

Chris Romer-Lee

66 saltwater sanctuaries from around the world

BATSFORD

First published in the United Kingdom
in 2023 by
Batsford
43 Great Ormond Street
London WC1N 3HZ

An imprint of B.T. Batsford Holdings
Limited

ISBN: 9781849947671

A CIP catalogue record for this book is
available from the British Library.

10 9 8 7 6 5 4 3

Reproduction by Rival Colour Ltd, UK
Printed by Elma Basim, Turkey

This book can be ordered direct from the
publisher at www.batsfordbooks.com, or
try your local bookshop.

Cover image © Dan Cantero/Alamy

CONTENTS

Introduction

The ocean exerts an inexorable pull over sea
people wherever they are – in a bright-lit, inland
city or the dead centre of a desert – and when
they feel the tug there is no choice but somehow
to reach it and stand at its immense,
earth-dissolving edge, straightaway calmed.

Anuradha Roy, *The Folded Earth*

Whether it's the walk along the promenade to find the staircase that drops over the chalk cliffs of Walpole Bay, the drive down the track to Tarlair Outdoor Pool (see page 11) or the walk across the granite rock shelves of Cornwall, tidal pools are etched into the UK's coastal towns. Big or small, thriving or dormant, there's something about these structures that is both mesmerizing and overlooked. Everyone knows what they are but have seldom stopped to think about why. Why they're there or what it took to get them there. Whether they are hewn from rock or cast onto a natural rock shelf these pools always solve a problem: providing safe access to water.

Access to water was a theme that emerged in my architecture practice, Studio Octopi, in June 2013. While on a family holiday to Zurich, I was encouraged to enter an open-call competition for ideas to develop the banks of the River Thames in central London. At the moment I received the details I was admiring Zürichsee Kreisel, one of many swimming facilities built along the banks of Lake Zurich and the River Limmat. 'Cradled in nature' was a phrase that came to me, one I used to describe proposals for a floating lido on the Thames (see page 8), and one I often revisited in my research for this book. Ideas were bouncing around my head as I returned to London. How exactly do you achieve a swimmable and accessible River Thames, and why would you want to?

As to the 'why?', over the last decade there has been a resurgence of outdoor swimming across the country and the world. Indeed, most of this book was plotted swimming lengths of the Serpentine in Hyde Park and pondering the significance of having safe access to water to swim in. Lakes, rivers and other wild resources are a welcome antidote to the unnatural indoor environments that leisure centres offer.

The restoration of historic outdoor pools has been a focus of the practice's work since 2013. The former seawater pool, Grange Lido, then Tarlair in Aberdeenshire and most recently Saltcoats Bathing Pond. Working with the energized community groups who instigated each of these projects, it dawned on me that this type of pool was no longer being overlooked. The unfettered joy to be found in entering sheltered tidal waters cradled by a concrete or rock enclosure, protected from the turbulent sea beyond the walls and yet still being nourished by rich saltwater and marine life.

This book, however, concentrates on the coast and specifically on community-serving tidal pools. By definition a tidal pool is a seawater pool that is naturally refreshed twice a day by the high tide. Most of the pools featured in this book fall into this category. However, there are those where the seawall was built too high, breached only by swells at high tide, and so a pump was required. Exceptions to the criteria have been made on the grounds of excellence, significance and irresistibility. Regardless, tidal pools should have minimal intrusion into the intertidal, and so wholly pumped seawater pools have been excluded.

Sea bathing became increasingly popular in the UK from the middle of the eighteenth century. Encouraged by prominent physicians such as Dr Richard Russell, who recommended immersion in – and consumption of! – the nutrient-rich seawater, the health benefits of the seas took hold in public imagination. The transition from inland spa establishments such as Bath, built in the belief that natural waters could treat skin disorders and other medical conditions, to the rugged coastline had begun. British seaside towns such as Scarborough and Brighton boomed, predominantly from the wealthy aristocracy looking to indulge in seawater therapy. However, travel outside of the established cities was an arduous task and it wasn't until the rapid expansion of the railway in the nineteenth century that seaside towns across Britain became accessible to everyone.

Beaches for sea bathing were selected only if they met certain criteria, much the same way that you might choose a beach to visit: away from a river mouth to ensure adequate salinity; stable beach surface to enable Bath chairs or bathing machines to cross it; and ample surrounding cliffs or dunes for the prescribed exercise after

bathing. Bathing itself was heavily regulated by Victorian morality, with genders split between different times of day, beaches, or even whole resorts. Once suitable beaches were identified a frenzy of building work began, transforming modest seaside towns into bustling tourist destinations. The phenomenon was quick to catch on, with pools soon popping up on emerging coastal resorts across Europe.

In Australia, the perilous natural conditions of craggy shorelines and an abundance of sharks have spawned over a hundred ocean or tidal pools. James Cook and First Fleet diarists record that Aboriginals in the Sydney Harbour region made use of the harbour for food gathering and recreation. The relaxed habits of the Aboriginals around water, particularly the nakedness, unnerved the colonial administration and various edicts attempted to control activities along the beach. The arrival of colonials pushed Aboriginal communities inland and their fish traps were adapted for colonial recreation. There are records of naturally formed rock pools being used widely by the early settlers. Plugging gaps in the rockpools was commonplace and often led to the gradual expansion of the bathing spots. An 1839 diary entry by Lady Jane Franklin (second wife of the English explorer Sir John Franklin) recorded that ladies were using a women's pool, Nun's Rock Pool in Wollongong, and that the military had erected a hut alongside the pool to maintain their privacy. In 1876, McIver's Ladies Baths was built as the first formalized pool on a rock shelf, providing safe access to the ocean with a naturally replenishing supply of seawater.

The Australian beach was always seen as the great leveller, an icon of an implied classless society: unrestricted, unsupervised, accessible by all. Within this public domain are ocean pools that go to characterize so much of the coastline, particularly the east coast. The use of ocean pools by Australia's migrant communities is encouraging and they remain well used among all the communities along the coast. McIver's Baths has seen off challenges to its important role in the community and become a haven for pregnant women, as well as those in the Muslim and LGBTQI+ community, bringing people together in a safe, social space.

Much like Australia, in South Africa the need for safe bathing conditions in treacherous coastal landscapes has led to the development of around 90 tidal pools. Most of South Africa's enchanting pools pop up in densely populated areas along its 3,000km coastline, but many too are the product of a history of racial segregation. Under the apartheid regime, 3.5 million non-white citizens were forcibly displaced and relocated in areas categorized by skin colour. In 1950s Cape Town, an inhospitable desert area known as Cape Flats was used for rehousing people of colour from the areas designated 'whites only' under the Group Areas Act. The enforced segregation meant that large swathes of the coastline became a patchwork of zoned beaches for designated racial groups. This resulted in huge disparities in the allocation of beaches, with non-whites being relegated to smaller, less accessible and often dangerous beaches. To provide safe recreation along the perilous coastline, several large resorts were planned and constructed in the mid-1980s. The grand Strandfontein and Monwabisi Resorts incorporated two of the largest tidal pools in the southern hemisphere. The designs were ambitious and flamboyant, referencing both the seaside towns of 1900s northern Europe and the cultures of southern Africa.

However, completion of many pools and resorts coincided with the collapse of apartheid, and beach fronts increasingly became sites of peaceful struggle and resistance. Multiracial protest swims, 'bathe-ins', and picnics on the remaining whites-only beaches persisted, with a major role played by the Mass Democratic Movement that used slogans such as 'Drown Beach Apartheid' and 'All of God's beaches for all of God's people'. By 1986 Cape Town had opened its beaches to all without waiting for government authority and by 1989 President F.W. de Klerk requested that local authorities desegregate all remaining beaches reserved for specific race groups. These mega tidal pools and their pavilions have a fraught history of racist wrongdoing, yet the resulting pools have remained embedded in the coastal landscape, offering refuge to all communities.

Tidal pools may provide respite from political unrest, but poor water quality knows no boundaries. From Kent to New South Wales, polluted water ravages beaches. Despite outdoor swimming undergoing stratospheric popularity, persistent coastal pollution is worse than ever, an undeniable by-product of climate change. In England, for instance, water companies continue to avoid accountability for dumping polluted floodwaters into the sea, closing off swimming areas and tidal pools. Globally, the bombardment of coastlines with council regulatory signage highlights how governments are attempting to wash their hands of increasingly polluted natural waterways. Despite pollution issues continuing to hamper outdoor swimming, there is now an even more resolute determination to embrace the outdoors, with the health and wellbeing benefits of 'blue' spaces widely accepted.

Beyond this, tidal pools are important pieces of social infrastructure. They are liquid piazzas, village greens, town halls and all the other places we meet and socialize. Far from being left to the elements, tidal pools are being bolstered by communities united through a common cause to restore, protect and manage their facilities. Now is the time to build more of these pools, both to encourage growth in tourism but also to ensure that access to water is there for all. In her essay, Nicole Larkin reveals how her analysis of ocean pools in New South Wales has informed the design for Australia's first new tidal pool in over 50 years. Returning to the roots of creating a place for everyone to swim, Nicole has designed a model for all future pools, one that is accessible to a diverse range of users. Studio Octopi, in collaboration with marine ecologists Dr Ian Hendy and Ian Boyd, have developed a tidal pool concept that combines habitat creation with leisure use. The pool is proposed for heavily urbanized beaches, with existing coastal development and no designated environmental protections and would build on work done to recognize and boost marine habitats in and around tidal pools,

putting back what coastal developments have taken away and significantly enhancing the habitat complexity. Using artificial rockpools within and alongside the main pool, marine life will return to the beach along with residents, providing a lifeline to many seaside resorts.

And back in London, our central concept remains providing safe access to the river, for everyone. The Thames has a long, often eccentric, history of swimming. In Caitlin Davies's *Downstream, A History and Celebration of Swimming the River Thames*, she records the rise, fall and rebirth of Thames swimming over the years, from competitive swimming in the river itself to leisurely floating pools. The last floating bath opened at Charing Cross in 1875. It was a 41 x 7.6m barge covered by a beautiful cast-iron and glass enclosure. The river water was filtered and heated before being pumped into the central pool. Studio Octopi's proposals were widely published because of the direct link between the ongoing works to clean up the Thames and efforts to reconnect Londoners with the lifeblood of the city. Utilizing a newly cleaned waterway for swimming has already been realized in Copenhagen Harbour – surely London could make the same strides and open a natural river-based pool? The practice remains optimistic that the link will be made by the authorities and Londoners will get access to London's largest public space.

From gender-segregated sea bathing in the nineteenth century to racially segregated swimming in the twentieth century, tidal pools are rooted in our coastal histories, often as the silent bystander to a dark past, but always there to serve a community and provide safe access to water. The breadth of users has expanded since the Victorians flocked to the coast and the inclusivity is stronger than ever. These liminal places bridge the space between a chlorinated pool and the open ocean, providing a dose of the wild in an enclave of safety. This book explores some of the most astounding tidal pools that can be found around the world and is a springboard to whet the appetite of those interested in exploring these natural wonders further.

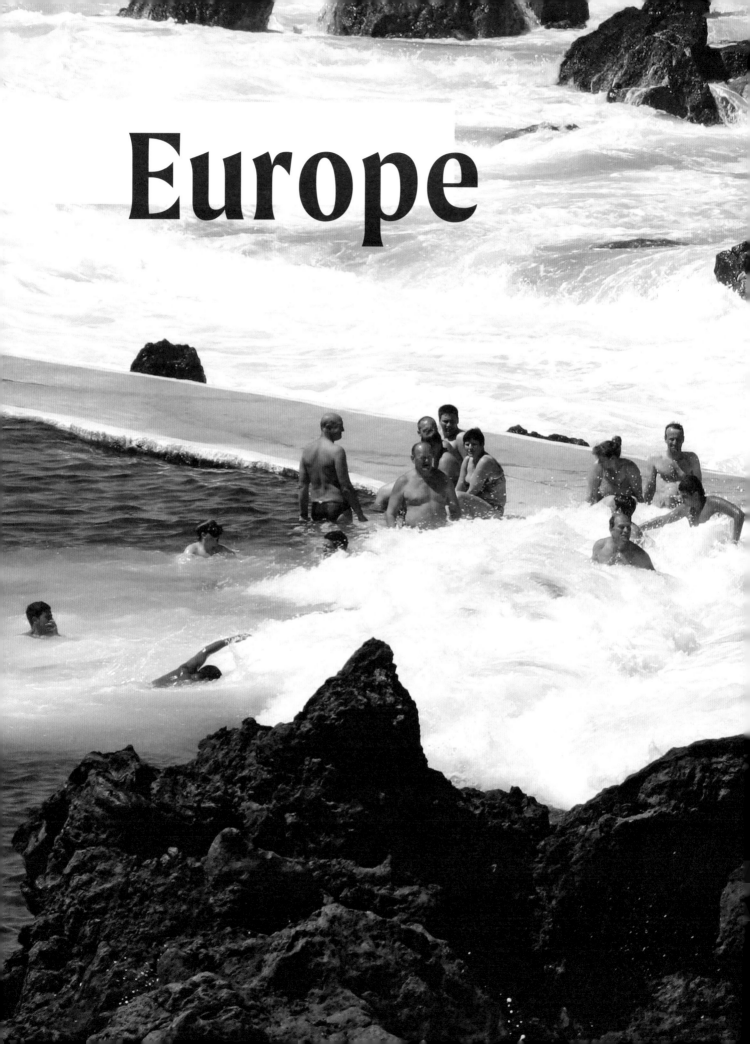

Europe

BELMULLET TIDAL POOL

Location Belmullet, Co. Mayo, Ireland
Built 1984
Designer/Engineer Club committee and Paddy McManamon (engineer)
Size 20 x 10 x 1–2m (large pool), plus toddler pool
Community Group Belmullet Swimming Club

Belmullet Tidal Pool looks like a 1970s utopian vision that should have stayed on the architect's drawing board. Thank God it didn't. This large cuboid mass, with the simplest of details, has been cast onto the beach. It is a rectilinear tour de force, more akin to an art installation than a pool and thoroughly engrossing to look at. However, according to Brendan Mac Evilly (author of *At Swim*), 'through time and familiarity the pool is no longer strange and unusual to local swimmers'.

If it hadn't been for a handful of strident female swimmers defying the male-only beach in the 1960s, none of this would have happened. They entered the water off the slipway, heading for a rock about 30m from the beach. The popularity of the swimming area quickly increased but, despite calls for a local indoor pool, the council never succumbed. However, Ann Maguire had other ideas. After spotting a tidal pool on a trip to Sweden, she partnered with the committee and a local engineer and drew up plans for Mayo's very own tidal pool. In 1984 the pool opened to huge success. The pool needs to be emptied and cleaned to prevent surfaces from becoming too slippery. This has become an important fixture in the town calendar because as the rising tide overtops the walls it creates a spectacular sight, similar to filling a giant bathtub.

I can't see this mass of concrete ever being consumed by the North Atlantic rollers.

CALHETA DOS BISCOITOS

Location São Jorge, Azores, Portugal
Built 1969

Over hundreds of thousands of years volcanos have spewed lava to form these sublime emerald isles 1,500km from the Portuguese coastline. The coast of São Jorge is fractured by deep breaches and coves, often creating beautiful natural swimming pools where the lava flow has come into contact with seawater to create curious geological formations. These ancient volcanic eruptions also formed the fertile fields where the vineyards grow Verdelho wine.

Biscoito (meaning cookie in Portuguese) is the name given to recent volcanic breccia terrain and lava fields throughout the Azorean archipelago. Calheta dos Biscoitos is the largest of the volcanic pools punctuating the coastline. These spectacular deep pools of clear water cradled by basalt volcanic rock were adapted for human pleasure in 1969. The new infrastructure, concrete walkways and bridges now allow safe passage between the pools. They were the first natural pools on the island to undergo these changes. Several bathing places have since been established along the coast to the delight of locals and visitors.

CALOURA

Location São Miguel, Azores, Portugal
Built 1962

In August 2019 two enormous waves swept into Porto da Caloura, engulfing one of the most enigmatic tidal pools in the northern hemisphere in a matter of minutes.

Despite the pool being red-flagged due to the tidal surge, locals and holidaymakers were at the end of the breakwater, enjoying the mesmerizing threshold of ocean and pool when the waves hit. Remarkably there were some minor injuries but nothing serious. The pool, encased in volcanic rock and concrete, survived.

In 1962, Manuel Egídio de Medeiros, councillor of the Municipality of Lagoa, together with a group of residents of Caloura, raised the money for a collaborative project with the municipality to build a public swimming pool at the end of the Caloura breakwater. The breakwater had been built to transport cereals and wine from Vila de Água de Pau to the capital city of Ponta Delgada.

There was already a shallow natural pool with some concrete steps, so forming the pool within the cavity was relativity simple. However, the concrete plateau needed to be raised by 60cm so that it was closer to the high-tide mark, providing a deeper pool and greater sunbathing area. The stairs were extended to the new height, iron handrails were added, and an acacia diving board was fixed to the breakwater. After 30 years of serving the community, the pool was refurbished by Roberto Medeiros, son of councillor Manuel, and engineer Luís Alberto Martins Mota, Mayor of Lagoa. Despite nature's desire to take back these pools, the community remains resilient from generation to generation.

EMERALD GATE POOL

Location Dinard, France
Built 1928
Designer/Engineer Franck Bailly (entrepreneur);
René Aillerie (architect)

Brittany has some of the largest tidal ranges in Europe, making it perfect tidal-pool territory. Typically, tidal pools are built on the beach or hewn out of rocks, but not the Emerald Gate Pool. Nestled into a former natural cove on the side of the beach, this gem has a commanding view over the sands below. The castellated promenade's serpentine form hugs the back of the pool, providing a fabulous vantage point for gazing into this oasis. Sweeping granite staircases lead from the promenade to the pool terrace, where the southerly aspect creates the perfect sheltered context. Aligned with the sweeping stairs, the remnants of a far grander diving platform remain. It offers a moment of exposition in this most sedate and tranquil of towns.

Realizing this pool took the determination of entrepreneur Franck Bailly and local architect René Aillerie. The council commissioned costs and a specification with the simple brief that the pool 'will allow sea bathing at any time and the organization of water sports events'. In 1927, despite not being complete, the pool opened to the public and instantly had the desired effect of extending the swimming hours. A 10m diving board was added in the 1930s but removed in the 1960s. At high tide all that is visible is the balustrade to the diving platform, while a ghostly impression of the pool's apron can be seen below the water.

English and American high society 'adept at sea bathing' flocked to Dinard and introduced the practice of water sports and tennis. A plaque unveiled in 1936 commemorates the centenary of the arrival of the first English residents. Picasso took inspiration from the area's emerald sea in a series of studies in 1928. It is claimed locally that Alfred Hitchcock visited Dinard and based the house used in his most famous movie *Psycho* on a villa standing over the pool, but no evidence has been produced.

ISLE OF MAN TIDAL POOLS

Location Isle of Man
Built Four tidal pools established by 1902
Designer/Engineer R. Archer and J.T. Boyde
Size Up to 3m deep (Traie Fogog)

By 1902 there were four substantial tidal pools in operation on the Isle of Man. Unfortunately, they all now lie derelict. These four 'ghost' pools have been included for their design, scale and ambition.

In the early 1900s the population of the Isle of Man was under 60,000 people. With the introduction of steamships from Liverpool in 1830, visitor numbers steadily grew before peaking at 663,000 in 1913. The island was considered a health resort mainly for 'cotton-ballers' from the Lancashire and Yorkshire mills.

Two of the four pools were built by R. Archer of the famous drapery firm Archer, Evans & Co. He was particularly interested in movements that benefitted the social, religious and physical wellbeing of the Manx people. He built baths at Port Skillion (Douglas) and Traie Fogog (Peel) at his own cost. Port Skillion was completed in 1871 and was destroyed by a storm in 1930. Archer's second baths opened in August 1896. Traie Fogog was claimed to be the largest of its kind in Europe when it opened. The *Isle of Man Examiner* stated on 24 July 1897 that 'the structure has been erected in part to meet a long felt want, namely, where parents with their children, young ladies with their brothers, relatives and friends, can enjoy the pleasure of natation together'. By the 1950s the cliffs had become unsafe, and Traie Fogog was forced to close.

In 1899 Old Port Erin Outdoor Pool (aka Traie Menagh Baths) opened. It was very popular until 1981 when it closed. It was converted into a fish farm until 1990 and then fell into ruin.

The last to open was Ramsey Open Air in 1902, designed by J.T. Boyde. *The Official Guides to Ramsey (1901–08)* enthused about the 'fresh water shower baths', 'comfortable dressing rooms' and 'excellent Refreshment Rooms'.

HAVRE DES PAS BATHING POOL

Location St Helier, Jersey, Channel Islands
Built 1895
Designer/Engineer Mr Lloyd and Mr Genge; extension
by R.C. Blampied

The Jersey Swimming Club was established in 1865 by a group of swimming enthusiasts concerned about the frequent accidents and loss of life at bathing areas around the island. In 1889, proposals were put forward by the club for the construction of two tidal pools, a pool for gentlemen and a pool for women, as was common at the time. Although both plans were approved, only the women's pool was built. In 1904 mixed bathing was permitted between the hours of 9.00–10.30am.

Havre des Pas Bathing Pool was opened on 22 May 1895. Built on a granite outcrop in the middle of St Helier's main beach, the pool is connected back to the promenade by a timber-decked walkway, reminiscent of a stunted seaside pier. The pavilion has the appearance of an elaborate wedding cake. At the entrance is a Juliet balcony to one side and a gatehouse with stepped pyramid roof to the other. Records state that various architects extended and altered the main structure over the years, including for the club's diamond jubilee in 1925. The pool itself is a sensuous shape, caressing the beach in a glorious and gracious sling of concrete.

During the German occupation from 1940–45 the pool fell into disrepair, and despite post-war renovations, by 1972 a new leisure centre had once again sucked swimmers from the wild to the tame. The granite structures withstood the neglect, but the concrete suffered. Happily, in 2000 the pool reopened after an extensive restoration.

PISCINA NATURAL MESA DEL MAR

Location Tacoronte, Tenerife, Spain
Built 1963
Designer/Engineer Carmelo Rodríguez
Size 60 x 20 x 2m

The road to Mesa del Mar isn't for the faint-hearted. Hairpin after hairpin finally culminates in a long, straight ramp, which happens to be the roof of Los Ficus, an apartment block in this small coastal resort. It took what the brothers of developer Arcadio Pérez Dorta declared an 'operation of madness' to access and develop this resort. But Arcadio Pérez had an ulterior motive: to find a site for his summer house.

In 1963, after a year of planning and with the assistance of fellow developer Raymon Wilfart and the architect Carmelo Rodríguez, development work commenced at Mesa del Mar. When Los Ficus was complete, they burrowed through the cliff to get access to the sheltered black-sand beach of La Arena.

Taking the full brunt of the North Atlantic, this pool is pounded by sizeable waves throughout the year. On impact, the waves leap the broad concrete wall, sweeping swimmers from the slippery top surface and tipping them into the pool. The seawall is at least 2.5m wide, with evidence of a balustrade on the seaward side. Small vertical posts remain, protruding from the concrete like teeth, ready to seize the unfortunate swimmer who slips on the apron.

Tourism dwindled in the 1980s, and the brutalist hotel built on the volcanic peninsula was sold off as private apartments. Now, there is a pleasant local feel to the pool and beach. Arcadio Pérez's defiance and skill in developing a resort in the most inaccessible and inhospitable place is valued by some and criticized by others.

PISCINAS NATURALES DE PUNTA PRIETA

Location Los Barrancos, Punta Prieta, Tenerife, Spain
Built 1980s; Güímar refurbished in 2000
Size Güímar 16 x 18 x 1.5m; Punta Prieta 17 x 19 x 1.7m;
Golete 7 x 13 x 1.8m

Even the satnav wasn't convinced that this series of small hamlets led anywhere. Yet, without warning, it turned up three pools nestled in these coastal settlements.

Piscina Natural de Güímar is a seawater pool set above the high-water mark, which means that during the calmer seas a pump assists with the water change. The tiny village of Los Barrancos stretches from poolside back along Playa de Callao and into a cave under the cliff. Over the last hundred years the village has evolved from beach 'huts' to homes without formal permissions. The pool was initially built very badly but was refurbished in 2000. It is the heart of the village and becomes a hub of activity during the summer months.

North of Los Barrancos lies Punta Prieta. Narrow paths between the properties wind down to the craggy rocks at the water's edge. Once again, the village has its own pool to facilitate safe swimming. This recently refurbished tidal pool fills as water breaches the seawalls but is also refreshed via a unique blow hole. Seawater crashes into the rocks, passes through the blow hole and replenishes the pool.

Heart-shaped Charco de Golete has undergone the least human intervention and is the simplest of these three pools. Prior to the 1980s, when the new seawall was built, another pool existed but it was positioned too far above the high-water mark. A basalt cobbled stair leads to the seawall from the concrete sunbathing area. You can navigate the rock edge via a precarious set of steel stairs.

These three pools, all in close proximity, capture the rich variety of this unique typology of pool. Each pool was built for the smallest of communities who now manage them, and each offers safe access to the ocean water while also providing a place to meet and socialize.

PISCINAS DE ROQUE PRIETO

Location Agache, Gran Canaria, Spain
Size 30 x 80 x 2.5m

The bay at Roque Prieto has been converted into a large, spearhead-shaped, twin-basin tidal pool. Like a prehistoric sunken forest, concrete trunks mark the seawall and pathway between the two pools, cast to protect swimmers from the powerful waves in rough seas.

A steep concrete road flanked by banana groves and greenhouses connects the town with the coast. Halfway down on the right is a niche cut into the basalt face. The Virgin Mary watches over the parade of swimmers. Accessible by just one person at a time, the cavity is neatly whitewashed and adorned with flowers. A single-storey whitewashed building with a window and door is the gatehouse to Roque Prieto. Stripped of all decoration bar a bright orange life-saving ring, these are ominous signs for any visitor.

The environment is barren and inhospitable. I'm confident any beach that might have come before must have been a bleak environment to bathe at. Instead, the concrete roadway opens out into a large sunbathing area in front of two conjoined tidal pools. The concrete of the sunbathing area eventually blends into the natural rock cover. Access to the nearer pool is via both a ramp and steps, while off to the left the bedrock leads to a small concrete plinth and ladder into the second pool.

PISCINE DE MER DE GRANVILLE

Location Granville, Normandy, France
Built 1960 and 1967
Designer/Engineer Auguste Gaugain
Size Granville 50m; Saint-Pair-sur-Mer 40m;
Donville-les-Bains 27m

Granville eagerly embraced the popular health benefits of sea bathing in the nineteenth century. In 1827 the earliest seaside hall was recorded, providing a base for bathers and a place to eat after a swim in the chilly waters. As was common at this time, the beach was divided for male and female swimmers. By the middle of the century a heavily industrialized Paris and new railway line to Granville meant an influx of wealthy Parisians.

One notable later visitor was industrialist and car manufacturer Louis Renault. In 1922 he bought the castle on the Channel Island, Les îles Chausey (the only Channel Island to belong to France). Located just 18km off the coast of Granville, Renault restored the castle and built a new tidal pool along its exterior walls.

It was another 38 years before Granville, nicknamed 'Monaco of the North' due to its location on a rocky promontory and burgeoning status as a smart seaside resort, opened its first tidal pool. Located on the beach below the childhood home of Christian Dior, the pool offered respite from the heavy seas and vast tidal range in the area. The pool features cast concrete starting blocks that are thought to have been included for use by the municipal swimming school. Each sugar-cube block has its number debossed into the front and side, with recessed handles for backstroke racing. The dynamic font looks inspired by the Futurism of the early twentieth century. At low tide an elevated concrete path leads first to the pool then on to a further platform with remnants of another enclosure built between the granite rock shelves.

The success of the pool led to the construction of two more in 1967. The Saint-Pair-sur-Mer pool is situated to the south of the town and features a

more elaborate starting-block design and a stepped plinth with a larger stainless pocket handle to the poolside face. Here the perimeter of the 40m pool is enclosed by a rope balustrade. As with all the pools in Granville, the wind hurtles across this flat and exposed landscape. Two flagpoles mark the corners of the pool, which at high tide peek over the water as though marking a shipwreck. Each carries a burgee with the Normandy crest. To the north, the ambitious Donville-les-Bains sits on the beach like an upturned wartime bunker. Two 27m-long pools are reached by the omnipresent concrete walkway. The first no longer holds water and is only around 60cm deep at low tide. The second pool is considerably deeper, however, the plug is out and the pool empty. It's still possible to climb down into the basin, where the ambition of the construction is impressive. The attention to detail bestowed on this pool is formidable. It appears to be constructed entirely from precast concrete.

These three pools in Granville are exceptionally fine examples. The increased focus on the detail and innovative precast construction suggests the success of these pools justified the cost of design and engineering them in such harsh conditions.

PISCINAS NATURAIS
DE PORTO MONIZ

Location Porto Moniz, Madeira, Portugal
Built 1940
Size 3,800 sq. m, 2m deep

This ancient cluster of saltwater pools was formed by the flow and cooling of volcanic lava over thousands of years in the small coastal municipality of Porto Moniz on the north-west tip of Madeira. These natural formations were adapted in 1940 with the construction of a concrete seawall that merged the fragmented pools into one entity.

The project was commissioned by the municipal administration during one of the longest-surviving authoritarian regimes in Europe in the twentieth century, Portugal's Estado Novo ('new state'). The serpentine curves of smooth, white concrete that provide access to the water are evocative of central European modernism that was becoming increasingly popular across the continent. In fact, concrete was an unusual construction material in Portugal at this time, but the regime was keen to progress its own style of modernism. During the Estado Novo regime, citizens were obliged to provide community service and it's thought the work to create the pools was undertaken by the residents of Porto Moniz.

Various updates were made through to April 1974 when the pool that we have today was completed. Although there is a small charge for entry to the pools, their scale and significance makes it worthy of inclusion. Further around the craggy coastline is Piscinas Naturais Velhas, which is in complete contrast to Piscinas Naturais de Porto Moniz. Enveloped within a lofty basalt terrain, these pools have high-level bridges and walkways for landlubbers to watch the more adventurous circumnavigate the pools. They're also free.

POZO DE LAS CALCOSAS

Location El Hierro, Canary Islands, Spain
Built Nineteenth century
Size natural pool 23 x 50 x 2–4m; artificial pool
18 x 30 x 1.6m

There is no vehicular access to this historic village, instead a meandering volcanic cobblestone path descends the cliff to a collection of *casas pajeras*, or straw houses. The village was established in the 1800s by fishermen from the nearby town of El Mocanal, and the traditional homes they built remain, although alterations were made in the mid-twentieth century when summer houses became popular along the coastline. At the water's edge there is a striking reminder of the power of nature that has shaped this archipelago. A black tongue of lava bleeds out into sea. As the lava hit the sea it solidified and created mesmerizing ripples that are still evident today.

Off to the side of the lava flow, the basalt cobbled street becomes a walkway that splits the natural from the man-made tidal pools. The man-made pool is filled by the high water breaching the seaward side but also by a large pipe that connects the two pools. The pipe also doubles as an overflow. Historic records suggest that the man-made pool may have originally been a saltpan, being adapted into a pool in the nineteenth century.

Despite the generous sunlight in the Canary Islands, the overbearing black stone that defines the buildings, paths and the surrounding landscape is lifted by the meeting of land and water. The waves breaking along this craggy coastline produce a white furore that creates a defiant contrast with the oppressive volcanic rock.

PISCINE D'EAU DE MER DE SAINT-QUAY-PORTRIEUX

Location Saint-Quay-Portrieux, Brittany, France
Built 1929
Designer/Engineer M. Ronaze (engineer)
Size 25m long

Quinocéens are blessed with one of the most remarkable pools. This pear-shaped pool has sweeping curves accented with an exquisitely designed, cantilevered concrete diving platform. Unlike the rush of diving into Bon Secours, the leap into the emerald water is more *gentil*, reflecting the character of this picturesque town.

That said, there's still scope for an audience. A large apron of sand forms the top of the headland, Châtelet. From this perspective the pool appears square, the tapered walls perfectly straightened by the line of sight and perspective. Access to the pool is from a grand staircase that plunges to the pool edge. All around are the emblematic white handrails that form part of the seaside improvements commissioned by the visionary mayor between the wars, Alfred Delpierre (1875–1957). To help deliver his vision, Delpierre appointed architect Yann Corlouër (1894–1980), who worked on much of the town's Breton architecture. It's unclear whether Corlouër had a hand in the pool, which is credited by the local tourist board to local engineer M. Ronaze.

The pool was constructed in only four months, which is impressive given the location. Initially there was a double-level diving board, but after a few accidents this was replaced by the one there today. Nestled between the pool and the beach is a further tidal pool. This one is shallow and makes a perfect children's paddling pool as it is shielded from the swell by a smaller outcrop of rocks.

SJØBADET
MYKLEBUST

Location Tananger, Norway
Built 2015
Designer/Engineer Norconsult
Size 30 x 15m

Developers often provide schools, parks and leisure centres to benefit residents, but very seldom a tidal pool. It was included in the masterplan to provide a landmark for a new residential area called Jåsund, but is also on the coastal path along the peninsula. This pool comes without tricks. It provides a sheltered and safe swimming area in an extremely weather-exposed location and the design has therefore focused on a basic construction relying on what makes these pools so great: nature.

This is a pool for everyone. Paths, stairs, bathing jetties and ramps provide access to the pool from several sides. The designers have ensured that wheelchair access is provided. However, not all visitors are welcome: the pool declares that 'should jellyfish enter the bath, there are rakes to remove them'.

SLIEMA
'ROMAN BATHS'

Location Sliema, Malta
Built 1907

Sliema was once a sleepy village populated by fishermen and their families. But the boom in package holidays and the arrival of hordes of tourists in the 1960s transformed Sliema into the densely populated town it is today.

Despite being called Roman Baths, these pools are most definitely not Roman. Although some believe they may date from the 1600s, the most likely explanation for their existence is that they were hewn from the rock by wealthy British Victorian sea-bathing aficionados who owned villas on the island. Many Victorians couldn't swim and yet believed in the natural curing properties of the saltwater. These finely carved and accessible baths are perfectly formed for nervous bathers wary of tides and currents but eager to benefit from the water. Gutters were cut into the rock surface so that fresh seawater, and perhaps wildlife, flowed freely between each of the pools.

What was ingenious about these individual tidal pools was the ability to cover them with a canopy. It is still possible to see holes in each corner of the pools where timber posts were positioned. A canvas would have then been draped over the timber frame, providing the necessary privacy for the prudish Victorians while also protecting the dippers from the fierce Mediterranean sun. Some older locals recall wooden rooms enclosing the baths to ensure maximum privacy. Men and women would never have bathed together, so it's possible that these enclosures separated the sexes. The design of these baths offered a degree of privacy in an era of modesty. In 1992, folklorist Arthur Grima recalled that up until the 1930s, 'whenever you saw a woman at the sea you would have thought that she had fallen in the sea as she would have been fully clothed'.

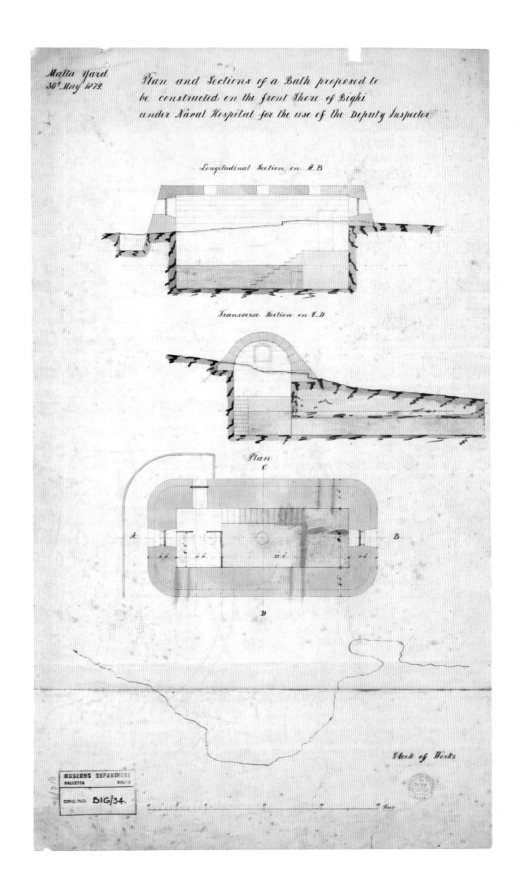

Plan and section of proposed baths to be constructed on the shore at Bighi under the
Naval Hospital, 1879

LA VALLETTE
BATHING POOLS

Location St Peter Port, Guernsey, Channel Islands
Built 1844–96
Designer/Engineer Horseshoe Pool, George Fosbery
(1844)
Community Group Vive La Vallette

A set of three tidal pools and a puzzling horseshoe-shaped bathing cove are sprinkled along the north coast of the Clarence Battery peninsula, south of St Peter Port.

The gentlemen's pool was the first to be built in 1844 by the parish Douzaine (council) to compensate for the loss of beaches caused by the expansion of St Peter Port harbour. This was followed by the horseshoe bathing cove and the ladies' pool, which was the largest of the three. The children's pool was added later. It took almost 100 years for permanent changing rooms to be installed, arriving in the 1930s, along with a kiosk and viewing terrace.

Guernsey Swimming Club erected diving boards at the ladies' pool in 1925 and the club held regular night-time swimming galas here. The evening's festivities concluded in the 'Fire Dive', where a torchlit procession around the pool ended with a bag of petrol being thrown into the pool, splitting on impact with the water. The petrol was then lit and a ring of fire formed on the surface of the water. A plucky local would then launch themselves from the 5m board through the ring of fire.

All four pools remain in use thanks to a tremendous community effort to refurbish them over the last two years.

VICO BATHS

Location Dalkey, Dublin, Ireland
Built 1896

Located along the affluent Vico Road, these baths
are part of Dublin's rich sea-swimming heritage,
with a history reaching back centuries. Like so many
places in the nineteenth century, Vico Baths was
originally a men-only bathing spot, with swimwear
most likely not required. Unlike the public baths
along the south Dublin coast, the Vico Baths
were privately funded by the Vico Bathing Place
Swimming Club.

Nude swimming still occurs at this tiny remote
swimming spot. Nestled in the nooks and crannies
you'll find many a local disrobed. If you needed
any reassurance, a handwritten sign attached to the
simplest of changing huts clinging to the rocks reads
'swimwear optional'.

Despite the nudity and cold seawater, Vico Baths
is a popular neighbourhood spot. At the furthest
point, the concrete path terminates in steps leading
to a tiny tidal pool measuring only 5m across. The
web of walkways and railings leading down to the
sea and tidal pool are the kind of facilities that
every rocky promontory should have to ease access
to the water.

United Kingdom

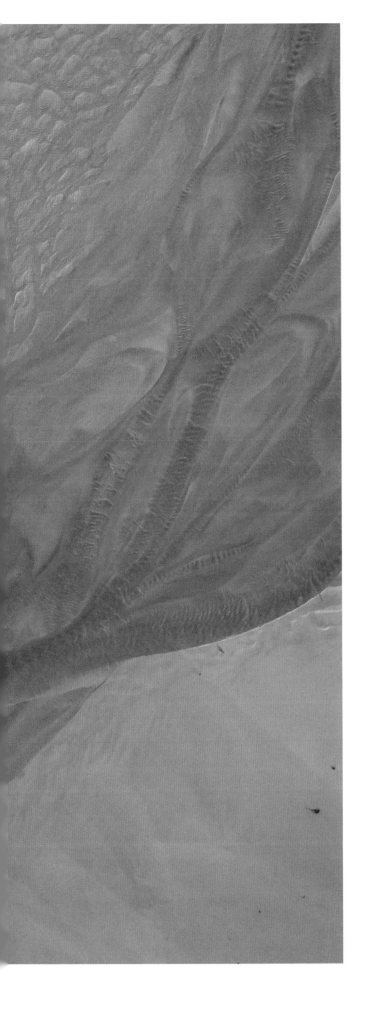

CHAPEL ROCK

Location Perranporth, Cornwall
Built 1959
Designer/Engineer Messrs E. Thomas & Co.
Community Group Perranporth Bluetits

Chapel Rock, or Chapel Engarder as it is sometimes known, is a large rock in the bay at Perranporth, Cornwall. It is believed that a small chapel or oratory once stood on it. This chapel, or rather anchorite's cell, was reportedly still on the rock as late as 1733. An account from E.W.F. Tomlin from 1922 noted there was evidence that its foundations were visible at this time. The location of the rock has long served as a breakwater protecting the village from the full force of stormy seas. However, the size of the rock has noticeably diminished as it has been relentlessly battered by the Atlantic over the years.

Nestled within the seaward side is a small tidal pool popular with both local and visiting bathers. The building of the pool was supported by local donations and Perranzabuloe Parish Council. It was first considered in the post-war period and was encouraged by the development of the Perranporth Surf Life Saving Club in 1957 when it became apparent that many residents did not know how to swim. The pool was constructed by Messrs E. Thomas & Co. and was in use by 19 October 1959.

In 1961, flagpoles were fitted on the beach and the flag of St Piran proudly flies on Chapel Rock. According to legend, St Piran, the patron saint of Cornwall, washed up on the beach at Perranporth. The flagpole acts as a reminder of St Piran's pivotal role in the county.

Despite the continual battle with the influx of sand, the tidal pool remains popular with families taking their children to learn to swim and use their bodyboards, and with a wild-swimming group, Perranporth Bluetits, who retreat to it when the sea gets rough.

DANCING LEDGE

Location Near Langton Matravers, Dorset
Built 1900
Designer/Engineer Thomas Pellatt, headmaster of
Durnford House

Rolling downs give way to a disused quarry and a 'ballroom-sized' plateau of pitted Purbeck stone. Here, blasted diagonally across the rock shelf, is Dorset's very own quarryman's pool. At first glance you'd be mistaken for thinking this was natural, but the precise edge condition and vertical sides suggest otherwise.

Dancing Ledge was the brainchild of former Eton College teacher, Thomas Pellatt. He converted a building at Durnford House into a preparatory school (later pupils included Derek Jarman and Ian Fleming) in 1893, and one of the rituals was a morning swim in the ocean first thing every day, no matter the weather. To make sure this was never interrupted he got a quarryman to create the pool at the water's edge.

A large iron grille initially covered the pool to keep the public out, but a stubborn storm soon ripped the cage from its fixings and returned the pool to nature. It is now accessible to all. Anthony Cook, on the *Outdoor Swimmer* website, describes his experience: '... The rock held me safe inside the pool, and then the waves began to come, skating over the ledge and breaking gently into the pool, showering my back with seawater needles. Wave after wave fell into the pool and broke over my head and shoulders, and, with every deluge that fell on top of me I felt as if I was being blessed by the sea itself.'

DEVIL'S POINT
TIDAL POOL

Location Plymouth, Devon
Built 1920s
Size 20 x 15m
Community Group Wave After Wave

Devil's Point Tidal Pool is Plymouth's last remaining tidal pool. According to locals, the pool is over one hundred years old, built in the 1920s. Located at the confluence of the River Tamar and Plymouth Sound, Devil's Point earned its name for the treacherous estuarine currents. The pool, a safe haven from the flow of the tide, reaches towards Drake's Island from the historic Artillery Tower (a designated ancient monument, built in 1537–39). Since the 1950s, the pool has been used by local Stonehouse schoolchildren to learn how to swim. Many of their summer holidays were spent exploring the surrounding rockpools that emerge at low tide and navigating the tidal pool's landing pier to go crabbing.

The Devil's Point tidal pool sits within a Special Area of Conservation and is bordered by numerous unique and important wildlife habitats. In recent years, it has become an increasingly popular, free-to-access place to spend evenings and whole summers swimming alongside resident seals, kayakers and paddle-boarders. With this rise in community interest, groups such as Wave After Wave have successfully raised money for life-saving equipment in conjunction with the city council and police.

THE HERRING POND

Location Portstewart, Northern Ireland
Built 1860s

A short walk from Portstewart Strand, a 3.2km sandy stretch of beach, is Portstewart Point and the discreet Herring Pond.

At first glance you'd be mistaken for thinking this pool was 100 per cent natural; however, on closer inspection a short concrete wall encloses a sheltered area of the craggy coastline, keeping the strong sea swells at bay. Atop the rock is a suitably well-stabilized ladder that once had a diving board attached to it. Exposed to the raucous North Atlantic swell, The Herring Pond has welcomed swimmers since the 1860s when it was rather more appealingly called Herring Pool.

According to Barbara Harding from Coleraine Historical Society, the pond has been the site of many capers and tomfoolery. In the 1950s, to conclude the annual diving display, the 'Fire Dive' was performed. This involved a flaming tyre and a small, courageous diver wearing a wet overcoat leaping through the burning rubber into the pool.

Portstewart and the neighbouring Portrush were popular holiday destinations for Victorian middle-class families, which explains the many other natural and tidal swimming spots in this area of Northern Ireland.

LADY BASSET'S
BATHS

Location Portreath, Cornwall
Built 1782
Designer/Engineer William Harry
Size 1.6 x 0.8m

In the eighteenth century the health benefits of seawater were commonly known. At first, drinking seawater was advocated by physicians, but then Dr Robert Whittie more wisely suggested immersion in these nutrient-rich cold waters. Scarborough began offering these revolutionary treatments, shortly followed by other coastal resorts, including Brighton. However, getting to the coast from the cities was expensive and time-consuming. In 1726 it took at least 12 hours to travel from Brighton to London. With the development of improved road surfaces and the railways, however, British seaside towns boomed. While men were able to bathe *in puris naturalibus*, a practice not banned until 1860, women, to preserve their modesty, entered the sea either fully clothed or in their voluminous undergarments.

The eight baths at Portreath were most likely formed in the light of this new belief in seawater. In 1782 Sir Francis Basset instructed his estate mason, William Harry, to cut baths into the rock 'for the pleasure of Susannah [Stackhouse], Lady Basset, and her young daughter Frances'. Sir Francis Basset (later created Lord de Dunstanville), Lady Basset and Frances lived at Tehidy near Camborne. After her marriage to Francis Basset, Lady Basset was said to want to create her own Brighton Beach, with hut and pool. The baths, which were predominantly square cut, now have a rounded, almost fleshy curvature to their surfaces, where years of Atlantic tides have gnawed away at the rock. Some pools even incorporated steps to allow a more dignified entry. It is thought that each pool is positioned at varying heights across the beach, so that at least one always had fresh seawater. Seven of the pools are no bigger than a large domestic bath.

LEWINNICK COVE HOUSE POOL

Location Lewinnick Cove House, Cornwall
Built 1927
Designer/Engineer Frederick Baker
Size 14 x 5m x 0.7m–1.5m

Frederick Baker, a wealthy lawyer and financier, bought the north-facing side of the Pentire headland in July 1910 with a view of building a Romanesque villa and gardens similar to a property he'd seen in Italy. Construction commenced swiftly and rock was blasted from the cliff to create a level base for the villa and terraces. However, the project came to an abrupt halt with the start of the First World War and, according to newspapers, did not recommence until after 1926.

When the house was finally completed it was swiftly nicknamed 'Baker's Folly'. It was alleged Baker had bought his land on the wrong side of Pentire Headland and as a result it only captured the sun for about three months of the year. Baker challenged these allegations by announcing plans to build another property on the south side of the headland with a tunnel cut through the rock, connecting the two buildings. This never happened and residents stand by Baker's north-facing home as a place that offers a uniquely intimate but safe exposure to the wild waves that pound the house during Atlantic storms.

Below the house's Italianate terraces, accessed by a short flight of weathered concrete steps, is a further man-made plateau and tidal pool. The pool is positioned just below the high-water mark and offers expansive views across the emerald waters of Fistral Bay. The pool was hewn from the rock and then lined with white-glazed bricks and turquoise mosaic tiles, probably imported from Italy. Despite being repeatedly battered by winter storms, which are considerable and dramatic, the pool survives. The house has now been subdivided into flats and the pool remains in private use.

MOUSEHOLE ROCK POOL

Location Mousehole, Cornwall
Built 1970
Designer/Engineer Harry Pender
Community Group Friends of Mousehole Rock Pool

Mousehole Rock Pool is situated below mean high water, nestled inconspicuously into the rugged coastline. The small, shallow pool is a tranquil spot better suited to gentle paddling than swimming. For over 50 years this community-led project has provided a protected and safe environment for the children of the village to enjoy the sea.

Wholly conceived and executed by a dedicated community, instigated by Harry Pender and built by family members and others, most of the money raised for the original construction came from a collection box with a brass plaque on top reading 'Children's Swimming Pool', located on the path above the pool. This, plus £33 left over in the village from the Second World War Welcome Home Fund, jumble sales and sponsored walks, all raised sufficient funds to get the pool started in 1969.

Nearby Penlee Quarry donated all the sand and chippings for the concrete; cement and equipment were taken down to the pool in a shop van; the north-east wall was constructed from blue elvan stone by two army friends of Harry on their holiday; children from Mousehole School volunteered their time to assist with the build. The blue elvan rock was blown out by dynamite taken from Geevor Tin Mine; blasts were so loud that at one time the lifeboat was called out and another a piece of rock flew through the roof of a nearby bungalow on Cliff Lane.

In 1970 the pool opened, with the works costing less than £1,000. The Friends of the pool are unfunded and continue to raise money for its upkeep. Recent restoration work and licence costs have all been met by the community.

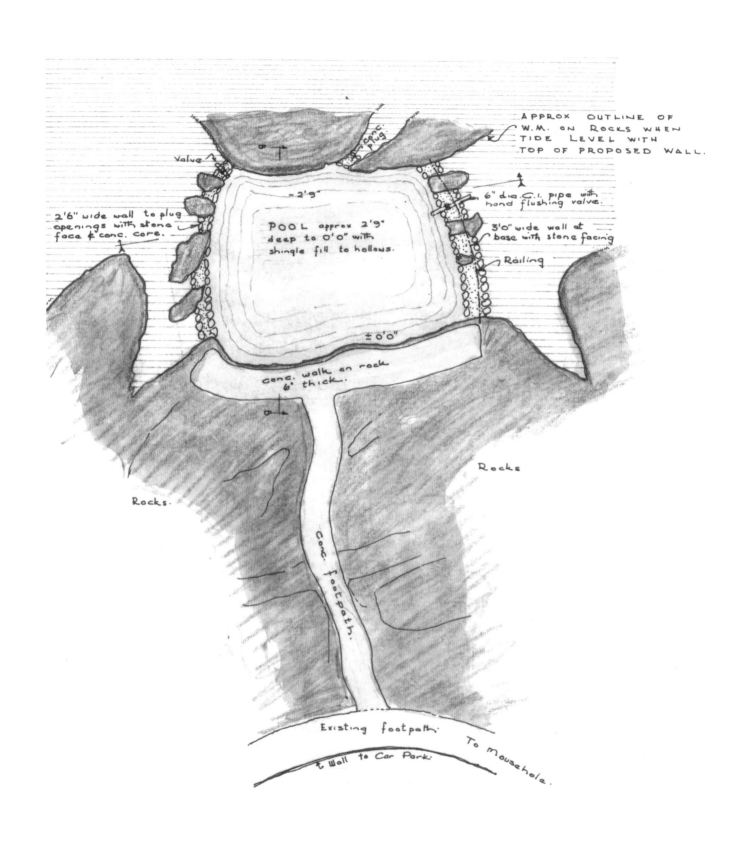

Above: Original plan of Mousehole Rock Pool by Harry Pender.
Right: Official Opening Day, August 1970. Sid and Janie Pender (top). Dougie Blewett (bottom).

The
Tidal Year

Freya
Bromley

I once read that all stories should start with yearning, and I was yearning for so much when I decided to swim every tidal pool in Britain with my friend Miri. My brother, Tom, had recently died from bone cancer and I'd just broken up with my boyfriend and moved out of our shared home – abandoning another failed attempt at starting again. Miri had recently been made redundant due to the pandemic and was looking for work and purpose. I was searching for something that would make me feel different, but I wasn't sure what it was yet. I thought 'it' might be a place. Then I thought that 'it' was quiet. The silence of escaping to the end of the Earth to stare out at the sea from a tidal pool, as though the deafening sound of waves crashing like cymbals on the coastline could soothe my grief for a while.

When I talk to people while wild swimming, it's not long before we're talking about the most intimate details of our lives: divorces, death, depression. *Keep swimming*, we say, *keep swimming*. I still remember my first wild swim. It was New Year's Day at Hampstead Heath Ladies' Pond. I saw my body differently when I looked down at it through that amber spyglass. The cold was anaesthetizing. It was such a shock that I couldn't breathe or think. I surrendered to the lulling shoosh-shoosh of the water licking the long-grassed shore and the tension at the back of my neck eventually released. Everything melted away. It was the first time I'd been able to escape myself in years. I've been addicted ever since. Perhaps that's why tidal pools seemed like such a good idea.

Our journey took us from a pool hidden in the cliffs of fishing village Polperro to the quarry lagoon of Abereiddi via Margate's sea-mossed Walpole Bay. I looked under the boulders of Westward Ho! tidal pool, along the limpet-studded edges of Dancing Ledge and in the dark caves at Priest's Cove. I didn't find what I'd been looking for. I still missed Tom,

but I did find other people that were searching. Searching for time away from the kids, time to be near others, time to exercise, time to make a community. And in searching, they found it right on their doorsteps. I realized that, more than anything, people are searching for a place to call their own. A place that will make them feel like the moment in time they're living in means something and that they have an ability to create some of that meaning.

One of our first tidal pool trips was to North Baths in Trinkie, Scotland. It was a Friday night in September when the waves pulled at their leash like a hungry dog. We met a woman in a bobble hat and navy swimsuit called Patty, who told me that in lockdown the tidal pool was her lifeline. 'I live just there,' she said, pointing up the hill to a smattering of houses behind a wire fence, 'so I can walk here in just me cossie and sliders.' She told me the pool was built into the harbour and that every year locals meet to repaint its boundaries. The week before the gathering, Patty will post on Facebook asking people if they have any spare industrial-sized condiment tubs, then collect empty 15-litre mayonnaise buckets to fill with whitewash. The volunteers all come together for cake, coffee and a swim in the newly painted pool. North Baths was a special swim because it symbolized a connection between women who recognized what wild swimming had given them in hard times. It's not unusual for tidal pools to be incredibly loved spaces. With every swim, and every stranger I met in the water, the challenge became more than just a way to explore the coast, but a journey of self-discovery.

Many of the tidal pools we visited have existed in some form since Victorian times and have had to fight against council safety regulations and funding struggles to resist closure after the decline of British seaside tourism. This was clear in Brixham, a colourful spot on the English Riviera. Shoalstone Pool is an Art Deco jewel on the Devon coast, but it lost support from the council after being battered in a storm. Despite the council giving up, locals didn't, and they fought to get it ready to open again by the summer season. Lifeguards and locals volunteered their time. Some did sponsored cycles to Tinside Lido and local businesses even donated tools and Alpine Blue paint, which can be seen on the pool perimeter and the changing room doors that swing open like in a spaghetti western. We visited on a cloudy day in May when the water was grey-gleaming. The sea beyond the pool was lined with red-rusted shipping containers. We watched them pass from the safety of our watery cradle and wondered what they carried and to where.

Miri and I encountered many forms of fundraising on our trip, perhaps none as inventive as the West Braes Project, which created a crazy golf course to raise cash for the required renovations to the Pittenweem Pool in Fife built in 1895. Above the pool is a large green field with oblong stretches of Astroturf that make up the holes. Each is sponsored by a local business or family. When we visited, Hole 12 was decorated with large blue and white fish for J. Doig & Sons, the local fishmonger in Anstruther. The pharmacy had a hole too, as did a local oatcake business, and Hole 7 – which looked particularly tricky – was a memorial to a man named Keith Grant. Beside the putting green was a blue shipping container with a bolted door that opened to collect change in exchange for a putter and ball. Beyond was the sea. All of it big and black and beautiful. The sun was so bright that the sea, and everything besides it, appeared dark and the light reflected on its surface like glinting diamonds.

Communities working together is something we saw at many of the tidal pools. It's not easy to find neighbours in modern life, and it's certainly not easy to make friends, but somehow these places have found a way to do that. Bude Sea Pool and Clevedon Marine Lake have created organizations to fund

their swimming spots. Friends of Bude Sea Pool and MARLENS (Clevedon's support group) sell tea towels, host events and accept donations, which means their pools can stay free and open to all. Their annual spring-cleans come when we all need a refresh. The water rises in temperature until neoprene socks can stay in swimming bags again. These drain-downs offer an opportunity to rediscover lost possessions from the muddy bottom of the pool. Someone told me that people have even been reunited with wedding rings from Clevedon's seabed.

Being on an adventure like swimming in every tidal pool in Britain enabled me to experience new places like a local. Explorations into the deepest and darkest depths of local archives, Facebook groups and internet forums connected me to strangers who quickly felt like new friends. People delighted in an opportunity to show me photos of their great-grandparents in the same waters or tell me stories about almost-forgotten places. 'Did you know fishermen used to throw crabs over the lido wall to help the lifeguard empty the pool at closing time?', one woman told me in North Berwick. These stories are passed down the generations. Some are nearer folklore than truth, like the heroic fisherman at Mousehole or witch trials at Step Rock, but the delight isn't in the facts but the act of retelling.

I saw that in the water too. As I travelled further from London, it became more common to see multiple generations. Grandmothers giving swimming lessons from boogie boards and grandfathers building sandcastles. Swimming, and its associated stories, is something that families can share. Meanwhile, I shared it all with Miri, and that felt special.

Our trip was not without complications. We'd set out to swim in every tidal pool in Britain in a year. The plan had always been to travel to Jersey, Guernsey and Northern Ireland, but time and money limited us to mainland Britain in the end.

Along the way, we swam in a few rockpools and later realized they'd been red herrings, not quite in our new definition of a tidal pool. It was only after we'd returned from a week in Scotland that we discovered we'd missed Saltcoats Pool. Perhaps the biggest part of the adventure was learning that it was about the journey, not the destinations. Before our trip to Perranporth, for example, I'd studied drone photography of Chapel Rock pool and was so excited for this majestic-looking rockpool on a biscuit-coloured beach. Then when we visited the pool was brimming with a foamy scum. It was algal bloom, the sign of a healthy marine environment, but hardly appealing. It was a disappointing visit that reminded me that these experiences were special moments in time. They couldn't be replaced; they couldn't be replicated. The trip was less about collecting pools like they were Top Trump cards and more about the quality time between two friends and rewilding an otherwise hectic life. I learned the names of wildflowers, seaweeds and the migration paths of seabirds. I understood more about tide times and coastal erosion.

Sometimes when people are looking for something, they travel around the whole world to find it. They hike for miles or climb many mountains. I read about a performance artist who followed people in the street for days, hoping to find a new direction. Hadn't that been what I'd done? I swam in 35 tidal pools in 12 months and hoped it would fix me. All that swimming taught me that I could travel far, or I could look at my local environment and think about how to make it somewhere I could find whatever I was looking for, whether that was peace, healing or community.

Before I started this trip, I'd been thinking a lot about a memorial bench for my brother and if it would be possible to find a place for me to feel connected to him. I thought about the places I'd been with Tom, then visited these tidal pools and found myself both further from him in distance, and closer than I'd ever been to my memories of him. I'd like to say I found him in each tidal pool, but the truth is that I'm still searching. Although I haven't found the resolve I was looking for, I found more reasons to live and a way to justify the time I have been given that Tom didn't have. Because really, this stopped being about place a long time ago and became about time.

You might be wondering how you can make your limited time on Earth special. My advice after this adventure is to start small, start local and start now. You might view your 'local' environment as the whole of Britain, or perhaps it's a little closer to home. Maybe, like Patty, it's even just a few metres from your front door. Wherever it is, wave hello next time you pass someone on the street. Think about how you touch the lives of those around you and the nature too. Pack a lunch, then sit and share your picnic with wildlife. Listen to what birds you can hear. Plant things in your garden that those birds like. Use your public spaces and consider your involvement. Is it comfortable? Could it be better, and if so how? Learn the name of a flower that grows on your walk to work. Water it. Read the dedication on a memorial bench when you sit down.

Freya Bromley is a writer living in London. Her first book, The Tidal Year, *follows her journey swimming in Britain's tidal pools. It's a true story about the healing power of wild swimming and the space it creates for reflection, rewilding and hope. An exploration of grief in the modern age, it's also a darkly comic tale of female rage and sisterhood. On her podcast of the same name, Freya discovers the human stories behind why we swim.*

NORTH BATHS

Location Wick, Caithness
Built 1904
Size 60 x 27.5m
Community Group Friends of the North Baths

The North Baths story starts in 1896 when the idea for a saltwater pool was first mooted. It was another four years before this idea evolved first into an indoor public baths and then an open-air saltwater baths. Despite reservations as to the universal appeal of an outdoor pool (again, on the grounds of mixed-bathing prudishness), the newly formed Northern Swimming Club persisted and secured the support of the Provost and council. By 1902 various potential sites for the pool had been proposed and dismissed. In what might have been seen at the time as a bold move, the council remitted the matter of the baths to a Swimming Baths Committee. The committee met monthly for the next two years and in August 1904, after five years of gestation, reports emerged that work to convert one of the many small harbours along the north side of Wick Bay was nearing completion. On 7 September the pool was officially opened by Provost Rae.

North Baths continued to be a mecca for Wickers for another 60 years until it was eventually abandoned in favour of indoor pools and package holidays. Then, in 2003, in a letter published by the *John O'Groat Journal*, Ian Sutherland described the pool as completely devastated but declared his intention of restoring the Baths. A meeting was hosted jointly by the Friends of the North Baths and neighbouring tidal pool, the Trinkie (see pages 86–87), who also offered a donation to kick-start the project. Over the following 18 months the community and business sector came together to resurrect this iconic pool through hard work and donations. The Baths were reopened on 24 July 2004, undeterred by the driving rain.

PORTHTOWAN
ROCK POOL

Location Porthtowan, Cornwall
Built 1908
Designer/Engineer Francis Beringer

Nestling at the foot of Eastcliff, at the popular surfing beach of Porthtowan, lies an intriguing, man-made rockpool dating from approximately 1908. This pool, one of the larger of the various pools that dot the rugged inlets of the Cornish coast, is well known and well used. It is sometimes referred to as the Mermaid Pool.

The pool is tidal and marks the head of the extended 1.6km sandy beach that stretches from Porthtowan almost to Chapel Porth in the north. The pool was originally reached by steps down from the cliff path, but these have eroded in places and now offer a perilous approach. It is advisable to wait for mid-to low tide and venture over the beach rocks, always watching that the incoming tide does not cut you off.

The pool was created by Francis Beringer (1855–1947), a well-known businessman in the nearby mining town of Redruth. Possibly in response to the near drowning of his daughter and her fiancé, he saw an opportunity to create the pool by forming a concrete bund to retain the incoming tide. Permission to build this facility was granted by the Duchy of Cornwall on 30 July 1908, dependent upon the payment of one shilling each Michaelmas Day.

POWFOOT TIDAL POOL

Location Powfoot, Dumfries & Galloway
Built 1899
Designer/Engineer William Tilburn
Size 34 x 28m

Under the big skies and silted waters of the Solway Firth lurks the relic of a holiday town that never was. In 1899 wealthy landowner Edward Brooke instructed William Tilburn, an engineer and contractor from Dumfries, to build him a tidal pool for a health and leisure resort to rival Blackpool. Despite being built in one of the least advisable locations for a tidal pool, a heavily silted and muddy foreshore, the oval pool was complete by the end of 1899.

The pool is built of large, squared timbers driven vertically into the foreshore that were originally held together by a metal strap. Once you'd navigated the silted foreshore, a cobbled-stone perimeter walkway provided some respite from the mud. At the time of construction, the pool would have been about 1.25m deep, with a concrete base 10cm thick. Unfortunately, this is now buried in the silt dumped by the 7.5m tidal range, one of the largest spring tides in Britain.

Tilburn initially costed the construction at £500 (£50,000 today) but the recorded final costs were more than double that estimate. Building the pool in such a challenging environment took its toll. Although the pool was widely used, letters to local landowner and developer Edward Brook in 1905 record the extensive accumulation of silt as an ongoing challenge. Despite the ingenious engineering to overcome silt build-up, with a split pool and two sluice gates, flushing the pool every week in the summer was a lot of work. In view of these drawbacks, it seems surprising that Brook had plans for a second pool at twice the size a mere 300m from the first.

With the onset of the Second World War and the failure to develop a resort to challenge Blackpool, the pool was left to the mercy of the elements and silted up completely.

SALTCOATS BATHING POND

Location Saltcoats, North Ayrshire
Built 1907-08 (rebuilt 1932-33; 1980s)
Size 56 x 52m
Community Group Splash Group

In 1828, the gradual decline of Scotland's salt industry aligned with an increase in sea swimming. By the 1880s there is evidence of swimming in the old saltpans located on the rocky headland to the west of Saltcoats town centre. Remarkably, the town is also home to two other tidal pools cut from the rock plateaus that surround the town. To the south of the old saltpans, a small pool appears on local maps from 1895 and a much larger pool was built in 1900 called East Bathing Pond.

The East Bathing Pond fell out of use after a bathing house was constructed alongside the old saltpans in the early 1900s. In 1932 the council decided to build a 100m, single storey pavilion and extend what was now known as the bathing ponds.

On 10 June 1933, Saltpans Bathing Place was opened by the Lord Provost of Glasgow, Alexander Swan. It was the largest tidal pool in Scotland.

The new pavilion had a covered colonnade at ground-floor level that opened onto an extensive concrete terrace with coved steps, slides and diving boards. Floodlights affixed to the first-floor roof terrace made this a popular spot for night swimming.

By the 1980s the pools, pavilion and terracing had been closed for some years and were in a poor state of repair. In 1987, the council embarked on works to make the site accessible again, demolishing the pavilion and terracing in the process. The Bathing Pond was also substantially reduced in size, with new serpentine seawalls and sluice. A curious concrete watchtower was added soon after. In April 2022, Studio Octopi was appointed by Splash Group to refurbish the Bathing Ponds. The computer generated image shown here is the concept proposal for improving access to the bathing pond.

THAMES
ESTUARY POOLS

Location Southend-on-Sea and Thames Estuary, Essex
Built 1914-30

The history of swimming in the Thames has been a significant part of my work since 2013. I've spent years attempting to cajole investors and London's authorities into building London's first floating lido since 1875. It was precisely the difficulty of accessing the Thames for swimming that led me to research ways in which we have historically overcome access to water in challenging locations. In the Thames the big tide, strong currents and, of course, poor water quality are all barriers to safe access. Yet you don't need to look far to find evidence of infrastructure in the river that ingeniously overcame these challenges to improve the lives of those living near a river often labelled as the 'lifeblood of the city'.

Heading an hour due east from central London, the Thames Estuary looms large. Along the northern reaches of the estuary is Southend and its associated enclaves. Famed for its 2.19km pier and associated bragging rights (the longest pleasure pier in the world), less well known are the seven tidal pools dotted along the adjacent beaches.

Council minutes from 4 March 1915 show that the borough surveyor was directed to proceed with plans for a 75 x 20m pool at a mean depth of 60cm. The construction of this pool, alongside the Crowstone obelisk that marks the end of the River Thames and the start of the North Sea, brought about six other pools east and west of this location: on Canvey Island's Concord Beach; two at Leigh-on-Sea; another at Chalkwell; and further pools on Three Shells Beach in Southend and just around the headland on the east-facing Essex coast at Shoeburyness. None were on the scale of the UK's largest tidal pool at Walpole Bay (see pages 90–91), but these were all precursors to it.

THE TRINKIE

Location Wick, Caithness
Size 60m long, 1.5m deep
Community Group The Trinkie Heritage
Preservation Trust

Trinkie, meaning 'trench' in Scots, is a bit harsh for this exquisite pool nestled into the craggy coast in the Scottish Highlands. As opposed to its neighbour and rival, North Baths, The Trinkie was originally a natural rockpool and maintains that special ingredient even with the alterations that have occurred over the years.

The Trinkie, including the children's pool, is longer than an Olympic swimming pool, yet there are no steps or ladders to enter the pool. The fragmented and jagged rock plateau that hosts this pool gently slips under another plate. Where the two meet, the high water is captured.

In the 1930s, led by the ladies of Wick Laundry, a series of fundraising events enabled alterations to this dynamic landscape. Concrete walls were added to contain the water at a greater depth but also to segregate off a smaller area for kids closer to the shore. Blessed with a sheltered, southerly aspect, the dark, iron-rich rocks warm up quickly and offer a very different experience to their exposed neighbour. As with North Baths, sluice gates were added to enable the pool to be emptied and cleaned out. Today it is cleaned and repainted annually by a dedicated team of volunteers keen to maintain the majesty of this grand pool.

With its limewashed walls and base, The Trinkie reflects all that was aspired to in the 1930s. Although the annual application of lime was probably done to ensure the pool's surfaces didn't get slippery, there is a distinctly modernist, Côte d'Azur feel to this wee trench, far north of the turquoise Mediterranean waters.

TUNNELS BEACHES
TIDAL POOLS

Location Ilfracombe, Devon
Built 1823
Size 50 x 20m

As the health and wellbeing benefits of sea bathing became increasingly popular through the eighteenth century, English coastal towns such as Ilfracombe rapidly expanded into seaside resorts. To entice the new sea bathers to the small fishing village, it was decided that better access to a small beach called Crewkhorne Cove should be provided.

In 1823 local entrepreneurs employed hundreds of Welsh miners to hand-carve six tunnels through the cliffs and promontories connecting the town centre with this water-locked cove. 160m of tunnel were formed over the course of two years of gruelling work. The pickaxe marks are still visible today, along with recesses where candles and oil lamps were rested. Today only five tunnels remain, with four in use.

The tunnels led to three tidal pools, a gentlemen's pool, a ladies' pool and a further, smaller pool. Unfortunately, nature has reclaimed the gentlemen's pool, the remains of which can still be seen from the beach. Each pool was set out within the natural formation of the rocks, with additional walls made from boulders and lime mortar to keep the water in. It took hundreds of men 18 months to build the three tidal pools.

Bathing was segregated and tightly controlled. A bugler sat between the ladies' and the gentlemen's pools, and if a man attempted to spy on the ladies, the bugler would blow an alarm and the man would be arrested. In 1905 mixed bathing was allowed for the first time. The opening of the Tunnel Beaches was a momentous event for Ilfracombe, transforming it into the resort town it is today. Tunnels Beaches Tidal Pools were constructed with private money and remain in private ownership. The pools are seasonal and there is a small charge to swim here.

WALPOLE BAY TIDAL POOL

Location Margate, Kent
Built 1937
Designer/Engineer E.A. Borg
(Borough Engineer of Margate); executed
under W.L. Armstrong
Size seaward end 137 x 92m; landward end 137 x 167m
Community Group Walpole Bay Swimmers

The decision to build two new tidal pools in Margate added to the already crowded offering in the town. The Marine Terrace Bathing Pavilion and the Cliftonville Bathing Pool (later known as Margate Lido) opened in 1926 and 1927 respectively. A further smaller tidal pool also existed off Marine Drive. The enthusiasm for seawater pools in Margate perhaps stems from the world's first sea-bathing hospital, which opened in May 1796, with the aim of helping poor people suffering from scrofula (a type of tuberculosis). Although patients received plenty of fresh air and sun, sea bathing was the main means of treatment.

The pools at Margate were officially declared open on the same day, 25 June 1937. Marine Terrace's waters covered 10,000sq. m, but Walpole Bay was an oceanic 16,000sq. m. The pool originally had two diving boards but they were later removed. The walls are constructed of interlocking concrete blocks and every few metres, old tram rails are concreted into the walls, running about 1.5m deep into the chalk. Each concrete block weighs about 1 tonne and had to be delivered to the beach and fixed into position by hand-crane at low tide. The work was carried out by day and night to take advantage of every tide.

Unique to Walpole Bay is the copious number of freshwater springs that discharge within the pool. The mix of seawater and chalky spring water perhaps explains the cloudy green colour and bone-chilling temperatures the pool always seems to maintain.

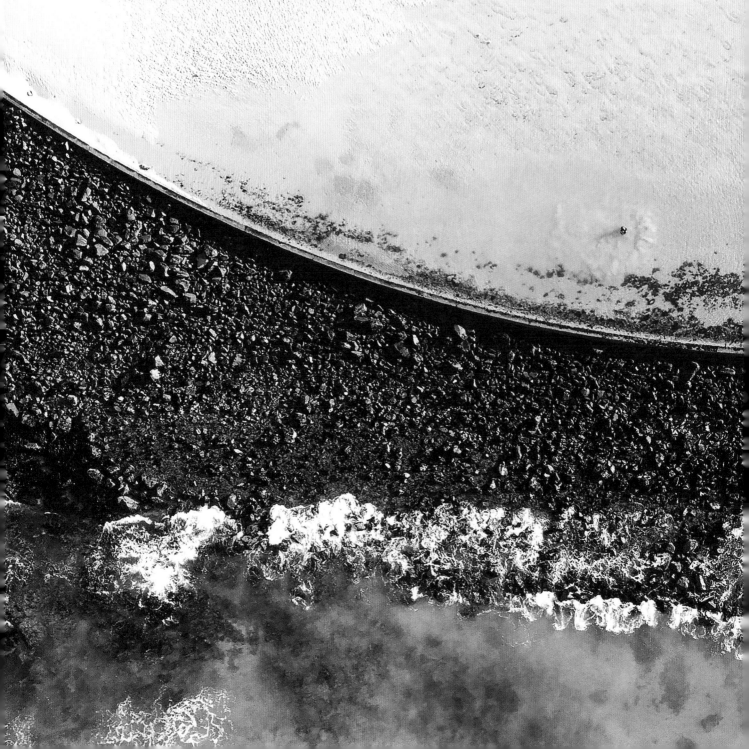

Africa

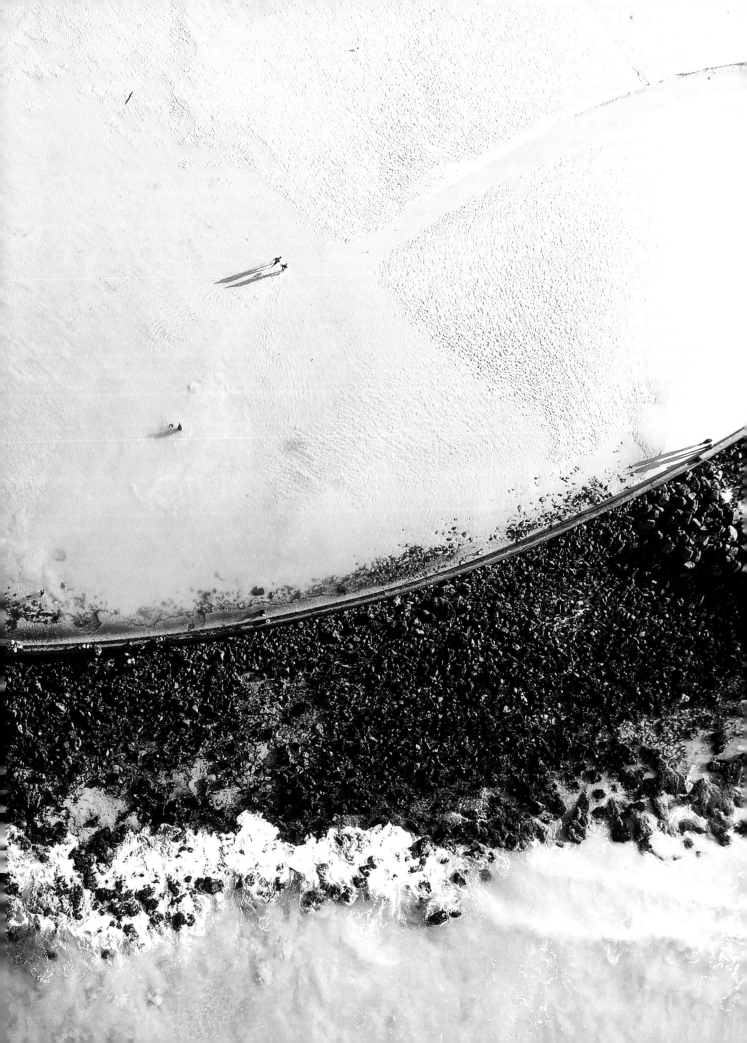

CENTRE BALNÉAIRE GEORGES ORTHLIEB

Location Casablanca, Morocco
Built 1932–34 (opened 1934)
Designer/Engineer Maurice L'Herbier
Size 480 x 75m

The three pools of Centre Balnéaire Georges Orthlieb are a place that the old Casablancais remember with great nostalgia and pride. This architectural gem had two stunning reinforced concrete, multi-level diving boards and an expressive concrete slide with spiral staircase and looping buttress. The slide surely influenced the design of Carpa Olivera's slide (see pages 176–177). At the time the pool complex was the longest in the world at a breathtaking 480m long and 75m wide.

Designed by the architect Maurice L'Herbier (not to be confused with the French film-maker of the same name), and inaugurated on 14 July 1934, this immense basin was built in the rocks, on the edge of the so-called 'Mriziga' beach, along the road to Ain Diab. The seawater was renewed daily by the tides but also with the help of a pumping station.

The pool fell into disrepair after independence, and in 1986 the pool gave way to the Hassan II Mosque, the second largest mosque in Africa, and the world's second tallest minaret measuring 210m.

DALEBROOK
TIDAL POOL

Location Cape Town, South Africa
Built First formal wall built in 1903;
pool augmented in 1907 and 1914
Designer/Engineer Mr F.B. Steer
Size 30 x 30m

This is one of the most loved and frequented tidal pools in Cape Town; it's also one of the most photographed, particularly at sunrise. Construction was started (illegally) in 1903 by Mr F.B. Steer. However, the prohibitively large cost of two walls meant the project was abandoned with the third wall still unfinished. In 1906, impatient for the pool's completion, 18 local residents, including the priest and postmaster, requested that the 'council authorize the thorough cleaning out and completion of the west wall of the bathing pool ... as it is noted that at low tide the pool was virtually empty with only small children bathing with any form of engagement.'

The council obliged and in 1907 the first pool on the Kalk Bay coast was completed and opened to the public. Efforts to improve the pool continued long after the first swimmers descended. In 1914 the pool was extended seawards by 6m, and the walls raised. The pool was then extended again in the 1950s with the addition of a curved wall, which effectively doubled the size of the pool.

Dalebrook attracts a loyal crowd from afar as well as being on the tourist trail. It optimizes the power of these places as a unifier, drawing together different communities and users, from swimmers through to educators teaching children about tidal-pool marine life. The incongruous proximity of the railway to the rear of the Kalk Bay tidal pools adds a further layer of engagement.

Dalebrook was quickly joined by at least five other tidal pools by 1922, all within walking distance of each other.

FICK'S POOL

Location Hermanus, Cape Town, South Africa
Built 1920s
Size 50 x 20m

As with so many of these pools, Fick's Pool has multiple conflicting narratives on how it came into existence.

More than 90 years ago, before the introduction of a high-end restaurant and the French Riviera atmosphere, the local school's headmaster petitioned the council to provide amenities for the youth during a particularly tough economic climate. Mr J.J. Fick had his eye on a natural cove located below his house that, with some substantial blasting, could provide the perfect pool. Due to the tides and exposed location, considerable works were required to form the pool. These included removing the angular geology within the pool and constructing a seawall that would effectively dam the cove. Once opened, a scattering of white-painted bathing boxes were added, and the scene was set. In 1965 the height of the seawall was raised, and the width of the pool increased to 50m, presumably so it could be used by the schools more formally.

Reports from the 1940s talk of death-defying dives from the top of the cliff just outside the seawall of the pool and dares to swim the wrong side of the seawall where sharks had been spotted. And yet, compared to its sister pool, the Marine Tidal Pool, Fick's doesn't offer much wildlife, likely due to the raising of the seawall in 1965. Nowadays visitors flock to Fick's for the Chardonnay and spectacular setting, but this pool has a backdrop of young love and adventure.

GRAAFF'S POOL

Location Sea Point, Cape Town, South Africa
Built 1910 (demolished 2005)

In 1903 Pieter Marias, a wealthy businessman, moved to Sea Point and built a house called Villa Bordeaux overlooking the beach and former quarry. Following the death of their only child at birth, his wife was paralysed from the waist down. To enable her to enjoy seawater bathing, he built a subway from the house, under the railway line to the beach. Here it joined a concrete causeway that ran out to the former quarry. As legend has it, he built the wall in front of the pool to conceal his wife's disabilities at a time when ill health and female bathing was kept private.

After his wife's death, the villa was sold to Jacobus Graaff in 1910. There's also a chance that he formalized the pool, or elements of the pool, for his family.

In 1929 Graaff gifted the pool to the city authorities for public use. No one is quite certain when it became an exclusively male domain. However, when the villa was demolished and replaced with apartments in 1959, the authorities painted a white line 2m inside of the wall. Men, who now used the area for nude sunbathing, were banned from appearing naked beyond this line. News reports at the time alleged that the banning was the result of complaints by the wife of a former state president who said she could '... see naked men from her flat, but only if she stood on a chair on a table and used binoculars'.

Graaff's Pool was demolished by order of local politicians in 2005. The wall screening the pool from the beach and town was its downfall. Laden with myths and stories, 'Behind the Wall', a short film by Andre Malan inspired by the stories, said the pool had 'served various marginalized social groups' and been reappropriated many times over. The film sums up the enigma of Graaff's: 'the excluded were forced to imagine what happened behind the clean white walls. Projections of their forbidden desires overflowed into conversations, novels and newspapers.'

HARMONY PARK

Location Strand, False Bay, Cape Town, South Africa
Built 1991–92
Designer/Engineer The Planning Partnership and
Interplan Architects
Size 300 x 150 x 1.5m

The Harmony Park Resort was designed and built at a time when the apartheid Group Areas Act of 1950 and the Reservation of Separate Amenities Act of 1953 were still being enforced, despite growing opposition. This took the form of civil disobedience where campaigners used beaches they were forbidden to use. In August 1989, Archbishop Desmond Tutu defied orders from the apartheid government and led hundreds of protestors to picnic at 'whites only' Strand beach. Less than 2km away from Harmony Park Resort, at Strand Tutu declared, 'We have proved these are God's beaches.'

Although Harmony was completed just as South African beaches were being desegregated, the fact is this resort was designed for 'coloured' recreation and positioned as a buffer between the affluent 'white' beaches of Strand to the north and the 'black' beaches to the south.

The sensory experience of the wholly man-made Harmony Park tidal pool is like nothing else featured in this book. With a prevalent school of great white sharks off the coast, the pool was certainly necessary, and the experience didn't disappoint when it opened with a sensory smorgasbord. Along with blow holes, concrete posts as 'wave splitters' were positioned along the top of the seawall converting the wave's energy into a visual and audible display. The designer described the performance as 'the sound of a riff played on a piano'.

Five islands across the pool feature plunge pools and fountains fed by pumped seawater. A raised seawall to the front edge means that it is never fully submerged by the tide; instead the perimeter walls to the left and right are lower and water circulation is via two spillways situated on either side of the tidal pool.

The pier is still intact, as is the majority of the tidal pool. However, nature is never far from reclaiming pools in such exposed locations.

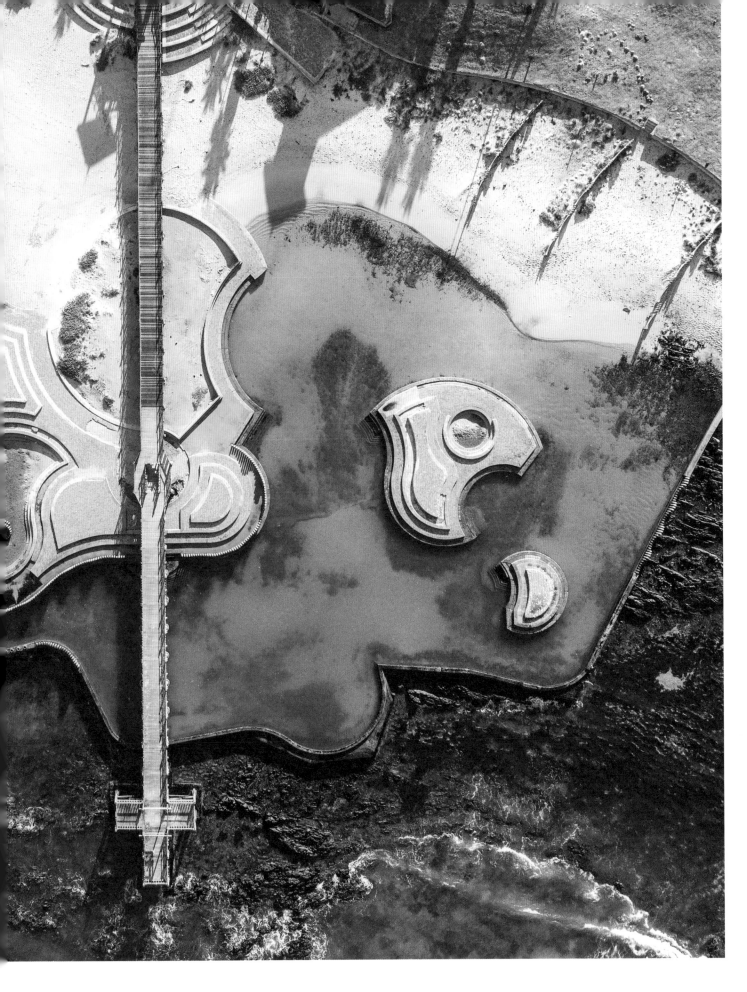

Time
and Tide

Kevin
Fellingham

At a few places along the coast of what is now known as the Southern Cape, low tide reveals walls of loosely piled rocks and stones, too porous to retain the retreating sea, but impenetrable to the fish who might have crossed over at high water. What they have in common with the tidal pools of more recent times is the relative calm of the water within, with the waves exhausting their power against the sheltering walls. Like the bathing pools, these were built to modify the environment in the interests of humans. They were built in the past for trapping fish to eat, which brings pleasure, along with sustenance, but it is difficult to imagine that the children of those first people didn't gain pleasure from simply splashing around in the water, or even floating on their backs in the dark and warm shallows, looking up at the southern sky.

Tidal pools make an interzone between the ocean and the land, they sit on the edge between things, and this gives them a certain charge, a hint of what would be theorized as the sublime – a place to experience the terrors offered by nature without suffering their full consequences – offering a state between exposure and enclosure. All along the South African coastline, children still stand on the edge of the seawalls, now made of concrete, often crumbling, and dare the waves of the rising tide to wash them off and into the pool behind them. Because of where they are, these children will often be predominantly of one ethnicity or another, one class or another, although increasingly those boundaries are being worn down, like the walls themselves, through the work of time.

The tidal pool as a type has two origins in South Africa, one ancient and indigenous, one more recent and colonial, brought over by the British to tame the wildness of the Southern Ocean, to make it into something more amenable to the idea of a summer beside the seaside. In the Western Cape, known to those who lived beyond its ever-encroaching eastern border as iNtshona-Koloni, formal segregation was established under British rule, and later hardened under the high apartheid of the 1960s to the extent that access to the ocean was to be allowed in one place or another only to one race or another, 'Whites Only' signs on the benches and the beaches ensuring that the pleasures of nature would not be shared, and that a mixing of bodies wouldn't lead to a further mixing of genes.

The desire to separate and to categorize, to exclude liminality, to close down the racial interzone, led to a curious collection of municipal facilities being built along the long shallow curve of False Bay, the almost uninterrupted beach running from the established holiday resort of Muizenberg, past Mitchells Plain and Khayelitsha, then a small township, now a semi-formal city in the making, on past Macassar, named for the origin of its founder, a political exile from the Dutch colonies of South East Asia, all the way to Gordon's Bay.

The pavilion at Muizenberg replaced an earlier, more festive building, and the resulting object sits in a sea of parking, mini-golf and a concrete ship, run aground on the concrete paving of an artificial paddling pool.

Ten kilometres to the east along Baden-Powell Drive, surrounded by the coastal fynbos of a nature reserve/buffer strip, stands the Strandfontein Pavilion, slowly degrading thanks to a combination of the salt air, the fierce gales and institutional decay. It is a masterpiece of post-modernism from late apartheid, designed by Vaughn Burns. It is, for all the aesthetic disdain and political revulsion engendered in those two terms, a truly fine, humane and exuberantly playful work of architecture. Seen in plan, it forms a long, gentle S-curve, centred on a vast, semi-circular sea pool. Standing on the cross axis between this pool and a grassed Greek theatre of barbecue terraces (apparently derived from a rescaling of Aalto's rustic staircase at Säynätsalo Town Hall), the main body of the pavilion steps up and back from the promenade in a sort of pantiled ziggurat. Now abandoned, it once housed a restaurant and function rooms, and must have been the setting for many moments of personal happiness, despite the public difficulties of the time, and the place.

Its plan draws on the influence of Roelof Uytenbogaardt, then one of the leading figures at the University of Cape Town. Uytenbogaardt was reviled at the time by his more radical students, not for building for the state, but for building at all, especially for those disempowered by apartheid, on the grounds that to improve conditions was to defer the arrival of the revolution (and shortly thereafter, one presumes, the arrival of utopia). However, Uytenbogaardt took the long view, believing that good architecture is a good in itself, and a good that would be in place whether a better society arrived or not. Strandfontein Pavilion is one of those ameliorative buildings, built by the municipality with funding from the state to encourage buy-in from the so-called 'Cape Coloured community' to a limited expansion of democracy to people of colour other than the Black African community – it is compromised, but it provided some happiness. Its present decay is to some extent a result of the expansion of choice and increased economic means that democracy has brought to its intended users.

Further along the coast of False Bay at Monwabisi, the pavilion and pools – built in a slightly more subdued manner – remain incredibly active. The township for which it was built has expanded into an enormous sprawl of largely informal housing, its growth driven by the internal migration of people from the Eastern Cape in optimistic search of work and better schooling, supercharged by the collapse of the industries subsidized by the apartheid state to prop up the Bantustan (Black homelands) system.

The last of this string of pools, that at Macassar (also designed by Burns, but in a manner suggesting the oversight of others), has been abandoned, its rooms slowly filling with sand, its roof being stripped by the wind and its paint peeling because of the burning sun.

So far, we have traversed 25km of South Africa's coastline, and encountered four of an uncounted number of pools. Each has a fraught history and happy memories attached to it, as does every inch of this highly contested country, with each group claiming ownership by prior occupancy, the same way in which we all feel we have discovered some little sheltered cove, only to be disturbed by another family who have been coming to swim there for as long as they can remember.

But what of those creatures who cannot articulate such a claim? The gannets, the seals, the urchins, the invasive mussels? There are activists willing to speak on their behalf, to point out that the pools are ecological deserts, that the walls distort the drift of the sands, that the concrete of abandoned swimming pools will be left after we are gone. They are right, but so were the first people who piled up stones to exploit the sea-life of the tidal zone. Should those people have known that by modifying the environment for their own gain they were initiating the Anthropocene?

I am not a great user of tidal pools – my first ocean-front memories are of a place sufficiently undeveloped as to make even infants take their chances with the tides and the sharks – but as an architect, I have always been intrigued by the way in which the builders of some pools have understood the stratification of the rocks, the result of their microcosmic crystal structure being prised apart by the work of time. They have cast their walls as continuations of ridges, or as perpendicular dams riveted into the fault lines, making a kind of primal architecture, land carefully reshaped to accommodate human use by proto-Vitruvian municipal engineers. There is a great pleasure to be had in walking out along those walls when the sunset coincides with the dying of the day's winds, when it is almost possible to forget that history has happened, and is happening still, that when the tide comes back in there will be the same sort of tumult as there is in the city, the country and the continent.

For much of the year, the pools are places of reverie, visited only by dog walkers and winter swimmers, many of them freed by age from the need to join the daily rush from coastal suburbs to the city centre of the industrial areas, but towards the end of the year, the patterns of use change, and once again they are places of intense and active sociability. Unlike Europe, Christmas and New Year fall at the height of summer. 'The Season' brings a tide of visitors, some escaping the northern gloom, many from inland and upcountry, a key injection of liquidity into the local economy, like a wave overtopping the wall of one of the pools. Their week or two at the seaside leaves them with the opinion that the locals are always at the beach, but this festive atmosphere is even more fleeting for most Capetonians. We have two New Year's Days: the first is shared with the rest of the world, but Tweede Nuwe Jaar ('second new year') is an artefact of our unhappy history. It was a day of rest for the enslaved people of the colony, and remains to the present a day of release, a day of heatstroke and splashing about. In the evening a train of tail-lights can be seen heading back towards the suburbs, leaving the pools to the municipal maintenance staff, and then, ultimately, for the small communities of more prosperous residents of the string of coastal villages to enjoy after the end of summer and before the start of autumn, when the rains reinvigorate the fynbos and the summer gales retreat, not yet replaced by those of winter.

There are no simple pleasures in South Africa: everything has a history in the remaking being worked out, economically, socially, environmentally and in the intersections between each and all the others. But the sea pools remain for the moment, many in decay, but all poised between time and tide, between historical pain and remembered pleasures.

There are no simple narratives in South Africa.

Kevin Fellingham is a practising architect and a senior lecturer in Architecture at the University of Cape Town. He lives in a house facing north across False Bay, so named for the False Cape, which caused ships to turn to starboard too soon, and find themselves unable to beat against the summer gales and round the actual Cape of Storms. He swims in the open waters of the bay despite a fear of drowning and a fear of sharks.

KING'S TIDAL POOL

Location Pennington, KwaZulu-Natal, South Africa
Built 1920
Designer/Engineer Carl Hall
Size 25 x 20m

Along the south coast of KZN there is evidence of at least three basic pools set within the sand and rock. Two are still working, one of which is King's Tidal Pool. This small trapezoidal pool is set just outside the lush landscape of Umdoni Park, which was established in 1918 by MP and successful sugar farmer, Sir Frank Reynolds.

Entries in a book published by the Umdoni Park Trust show that in June 1918 Reynolds worked with a civil engineer and surveyor named Carl Hall to identify a good place for a swimming pool.

By January 1920, '... the ladies' dressing room had been in hand for some two weeks, and the last rocks blasted away to allow high tide to fill the pool'.

Reynolds, who become a close friend of General Louis Botha (first prime minister of South Africa), delighted his friend when he transferred the land into a trust with the clause that the estate's significant property, Botha House, be left to the prime minister and his successors. Within the trust deeds is a specific clause that stipulates the trustees are responsible for the 'maintenance and upkeep of the Bathing Pool and Golf Course'. Although General Botha died before completion of the property, his wife lived there until her death in 1937.

Records show that Annie Botha enjoyed the pool, and its remote and wild location made it a good place to witness crabs, fish and all kinds of sea life along this stretch of coastline.

LANGSTRAND TIDAL POOL

Location Langstrand, Namibia
Built 1987
Designer Johan van Papendorp (OVP)
and GFJ Engineers
Size 4,000 sq. m, up to 2m deep

Along the entire 1,500km Atlantic coast north of Cape Town to Swakopmund there are only three tidal pools. By far the largest and most impressive is the tidal pool and jetty at Langstrand.

Langstrand is a small beach resort situated about halfway along the coastal road between Walvis Bay and Swakopmund. Here the Namib Desert meets the Atlantic Ocean in raucous fashion. Strong emerald surges crash into a mix of rock and fragile desert sands, making swimming conditions precarious for the young and old.

The resort was established when Walvis Bay was still an exclave of the Republic of South Africa surrounded by the territory of South West Africa (which had been a German colony up to the First World War), to lure more tourism to the area. At the northernmost tip of the resort is the 150m long fishing jetty and tidal pool, which is part of a sprawling geometric landscape, including parking and picnic area. From the air the design is reminiscent of a long-forgotten *Star Wars* film set. Astrological influences, arcs and diagonals dance their way up the coastline from a pivot point created from the line of the jetty meeting a circular public *platz*. Of particular interest are the three smaller circular pools within the tidal pool. Offset concrete arcs allow for steps down into shallow paddling pools. The pools terrace down to the tidal pool, which has a sandy sloping base to a depth of 2m. The pool is connected to a 3,000sq. m artificial lagoon designed to take excess water from waves overtopping into the pool. This was designed by Eddie Bosman and is unique to Langstrand pool.

MONWABISI

Location Khayelitsha, Cape Town, South Africa
Built 1986
Designer/Engineer Graham Parker (GAPP Architects)
Size 260 x 150m at its furthest points

This outrageously large, kidney-shaped pool is a contender for the largest tidal pool in the southern hemisphere, the other being Strandfontein (see pages 120–121). It even has its own island.

This monumental pool – and totally out-of-scale pavilion – was designed by architect Graham Parker for the city of Cape Town as the centrepiece of the Monwabisi Resort. Established in 1986, the resort was completed when the policy of apartheid was still in place. Monwabisi was one of two resorts built for the relocated 'black' communities of Khayelitsha on the Cape Flats, the irony being that the resort was only accessible by bus or taxi as most of the population couldn't afford their own transport. The apartheid authorities didn't choose the location for Monwabisi (meaning 'the entertainer' in Xhosa) as a convenience for the community – instead, because the area was contained within two natural barriers, visitors were easily screened from the adjacent resorts. In his essay *Separate Amenities*, Vincent Bezuidenhout states that the patronizing 'fun and fantasy' language of the architecture on the site was in direct contrast to its grander neighbour, Muizenberg Pavilion, which was designed by the same architect at the same time for 'white' recreation.

Building a pool of this size poses all sorts of issues, especially considering the northern beaches of the False Bay coastline experience higher waves with more velocity than the southern beaches.

Upon opening it was noticed that waves breaching the seawall caused an uneven base to the pool. It was reported swimmers descended from waist-deep water to a 2m drop in a single step. To overcome the numerous problems created by the pool, the authorities built a 170m breakwater off the seaward wall of the tidal pool and a short groyne on the beach. The problems were solved in the tidal pool, however the waters the other side of the breakwater remain, with riptides able to sweep swimmers out to sea. The decision to build a pool of this size in this location, given what was known about the beach, remains questionable and possibly dictated by politics rather than the safety of the community.

1. The central pavilion and br[...]
South Eastern winds by a semi[...]
2. During peak season crowds[...]
3. Turrets, kiosks and viewing[...]
fiberglass, architectural featur[...]
4, 5, 6. Innovative detailing f[...]
blockwork, timber fins, plaster[...]
tower.
7, 8. Both the gateway to and[...]
American and Colonial, styles[...]
9. Bright sculptural landmark[...]

poles set the stage for a memorable day at the sea.

10, 11. Vying for attention with the turquoise sea and the primary coloured pavilions are the murals painted by artists from the Nyanga Art Centre. Their deep sense of fun and originality — swimmers on a wall of sea, brightly skirted dancing girls and troupes of musicians — add to a fun filled atmosphere.

12, 13. Even the normally mundane areas such as toilets, showers and open air changing facilities are imbued with a "Raiders of the Lost Ark" quality.

14. The tidal pool, the largest in Africa, was constructed at a cost of R3-million to provide safe bathing to a section of the coast which is often dangerous.

15. A view from the west shows the terraced amphitheatre, west pavilion and life-savers' tower in the distance. All three nodes are linked by a sheltered promenade.

SALT ROCK
TIDAL POOL

Location Salt Rock, KwaZulu-Natal, South Africa
Built 1940s
Designer/Engineer Basil Hulett

A century ago, Salt Rock was dotted with humble sugar-cane farms and beachside cottages. By 1930 Basil Hulett had become the biggest sugar-cane farmer in KZN and his success – and influx of money – transformed Salt Rock into a bustling town.

Hulett first built a nine-hole golf course, shortly followed by the 1933 Salt Rock Hotel, designed to accommodate the steady stream of golfers descending on the small coastal town. The hotel's success soon exceeded that of the farm and he sold up, shifting his focus to redeveloping the coastline. With the revenue from the sale of beachside plots he purchased the beach in front of the hotel from the fisheries department and set about the construction of the curiously shaped tidal pool.

There are no records explaining why the shape resembles the head of a wrench; it could quite simply be because of the rock topology. The pool, complete with an unusual bridge and combination of rock and concrete walls, was not the instant hit Hulett had hoped for, since it turned out that most of his clientele had never learned to swim. Undeterred, the entrepreneurial hotelier fixed a hawser between two of the fisherman's towers that were integral to the design of the pool. From the hawser he extended a rope into the tidal pool, which guests could use to hold on to. His ingenuity did the trick, and the tidal pool became a success.

ST JAMES TIDAL POOL

Location Cape Town, South Africa
Built First wall 1911; additions in 1913 and 1923
Size 30 x 15m
Community Group The Beach Co-op

Approaching St James along Danger Beach it's the rainbow coloured beach huts, reminiscent of English seaside towns, that punctuate the coastline. Out in front, the tidal pool lunges into the sea and is quite a sight to behold. Situated on the site of an age-old Khoisan fish trap, the not-quite-perpendicular seawalls seem to exaggerate the perspective of this pool. But St James is not featured for its geometry – it is what happens below the surface that is a revelation.

My conversation with adrenaline junkie turned free diver and environmentalist Lisa Beasley starts with my ill-advised admiration for her favourite pool's whitewashed edges. I'm rightly slapped down. Lisa is a fierce advocate for the conservation of the natural ecology in Cape Town's Kalk Bay pools, and painting the pool surrounds in a toxic paint is her latest battle. The tidal pools were being drained every month and cleaned with copper sulphate or chlorine. Lisa, with the encouragement of St James regulars, crowdfunded a pump and jet washer and convinced the authorities to use seawater to remove algal growth on the top surface of the seawalls and to never drain St James, Dalebrook (see pages 96–97) and Wooley's (see pages 122–123). St James has now embraced full eco, whereas Dalebrook persists with a purely aesthetic application.

The success of Lisa's work has not only raised the profile of the pools but also increased their reach into the wider community. Through The Beach Co-op, she has illuminated what lies below the water's surface to kids and the dialogues about the species inhabiting the pools have bloomed above the water. The habitats below the waterline have gone from strength to strength.

STRANDFONTEIN

Location Strandfontein, Cape Town, South Africa
Built 1983
Designer/Engineer Vaughn Burns (architect)
Size 300 x 130 x 1.2m (maximum)

There is nothing quite like Strandfontein. Not content with being one of the largest tidal pools in the southern hemisphere, it boasts a magnificent postmodern pavilion that envelops its 300m length. The bitter 'south-easter' winds and perilous current are no match for this brute.

During the apartheid era the resort was zoned for exclusive use by 'coloureds' from the Cape Town flats, and the communities from the townships still make up many of the users of the beach-front amenities. The pavilion is civic in its approach, housing lifesaving teams, changing rooms, restaurants and more. The linear building is punctuated along its length, looking one way to the oceanic scaled pool and the other to the sheltered grassed dunes. Nestled into the dunes on the leeward side is an open-air concert space. The building uses colour sparingly, leaning towards the traditional white walls of the Cape, but where it explodes into life it is a postmodern masterpiece of contrasting textures and patterns. Like so much of this pavilion, the architecture has turned this windswept and inhospitable terrain into something truly magical, although the exposed location is taking its toll.

The vast sandy pool is an altogether more tranquil affair, with fishermen continuing the heritage of the site as a fish trap, casting from the boundary wall into the expansive ocean beyond.

WOOLEY'S POOL

Location Kalk Bay, Cape Town, South Africa
Built 1912
Size 20 x 10m

Devoid of broad, sandy beaches and scored by a
steady stream of trains passing on the nearby railway
line, Wooley's Pool is far from tranquil. However,
this charming pool is truly mesmerizing. It appears
to have quite literally appeared from within the
rock bed. Minor human improvements have been
made to dam the mouth of the gully and to improve
the perimeter edges, but the beauty of this pool is
its organic simplicity, evocative of Cornish miners'
pools. A small, shallow pool was added for children
to splash around in.

The white decoration appears to emanate from
the pool, spilling out onto surrounding areas.
The painted pool base turns the water an enticing
turquoise. However, the whitewashed pool is a
startling reminder that this is not a natural pool. In
fact, the whitewash is a toxic mix that does nothing
for the pool's ecosystem.

Australia

AVALON ROCKPOOL

Location Avalon, New South Wales
Built 1921
Designer/Engineer A.J. Small
Size 25 x 17m

In 1921 Arthur Jabez Small, a businessman and developer, purchased land from a larger Irish Jesuit-owned estate, subdivided it, and named the area Avalon. The first subdivision was the Palmgrove Estate and local newspaper advertisements show the rockpool alongside the beach. In keeping with Small's vision of Avalon as an 'earthly paradise', he lodged a cheque with Warringah Shire Council for the existing 'Bathing Pool' to be formalized.

The pool resembled a natural pool, with huge boulders around its edge. These both limited accessibility and, due to their distance below the high-water mark, provided a continual danger of waves entering the pool. The historic photos illustrate the wild and natural feel of the original bathing pool. Small's alterations in 1922 extended the pool a further 5.5m to its current size. In 1939 the children's pool was added.

To preserve the beauty of the area, Small placed a covenant on the subdivision of the plot to ensure minimum block sizes and prevent unnecessary removal of trees. This led to an area with a unique architectural approach where well-known architects designed houses linked to the natural surroundings, American-born architect Walter Burley Griffin's Stella James House from 1933–34 being the most famous.

BLUE POOL

Location Bermagui, New South Wales
Built Formalized in 1938
Size 61 x 30m
Community Group Bermagui Blue Balls (men);
Blue Pointers (ladies); Bluebottles (children)

The natural bathing spot called the Blue Pool was formalized as a swimming pool thanks to the vision of philanthropist Bill Dickinson. Bill moved to Bermagui in 1935 after a visit to the town's cemetery, where he noticed many of the locals lived well into their eighties. Bill never bought anywhere and lived in the Horseshoe Bay Hotel for 15 years until his death in December 1950.

During this period Bill funded, wholly or partially, several civic projects that aimed to beautify Bermagui. Upgrading the Blue Hole to a pool reflected the increase in competitive swimming in Australia and the relaxing of rules surrounding segregation in competitive swimming. Soon after his arrival in the town he initiated the project. A visit to Bermagui by the NSW Minister for Works and Local Government culminated in a grant of 200 Australian pounds and, with generous support from the local community who raised almost the equivalent, the pool reopened in 1938.

The delicate casting of concrete knits the natural rock borders together. The emerald water shimmers on the rocky base, and the abundant natural habitat makes this a very special place that sits with a handful of other pools bridging the divide between man-made and natural.

Dickinson was nicknamed 'Lord Nuffield of Bermagui' because of his local philanthropy, although, unlike his English counterpart, he had no connection to the motor vehicle – quite the opposite, and his commitment to the health and wellbeing of Bermagui isn't forgotten. In addition to the improvements to the pool, Dickinson funded the town's tennis courts and cricket pavilion. His use of local labour during the Depression era is still applauded within the vicinity.

Next-Generation Ocean Pools

Nicole
Larkin

The coastline is deeply important to Australians old and new. It is part of our national psyche and cultural identity; we see ourselves as a nation of beachgoers and coastal dwellers. In the state of New South Wales alone, we enjoy over 120 ocean and harbour pools – more than any other stretch of coast in the world. If our surroundings speak of who we are, in Australia, ocean pools tell of a love affair with the water's edge.

Our foreshores and intertidal areas are first and foremost the lands of our Indigenous people, who hold a deep and unbroken connection to Sea Country. Many ocean pools began as coastal fish traps with deep histories that stretch back millennia. More recently our ocean pools have served the community for over 200 years and have become a touchstone for our ongoing affinity with the coast. Today they are enjoying a high-profile revival in Australia and abroad thanks to their photogenic presence on social media and free public access.

Ocean pools are a distinct and much-loved part of civic life and beach culture in the east coast state of New South Wales. They're understated and unassuming, framed against rock platforms, the surf and the tides. These pools inspire myriad ways to experience the ocean. They expand the definition of what a pool is and who can use it. They cater for a variety of people in the community, from hard-core winter swimmers to chain-surfing teens, and those who seek out female-only bathing. In Australia, the beach is sometimes described as the great leveller and in the case of ocean pools this holds true. They are enjoyed by all walks (and species) of life.

Ocean pools in NSW also have a rich tradition of being initiated by the community, for the community. Many pools were originally built in the post-Depression years as public works projects, commissioned to stimulate jobs. They were started by entrepreneurial municipal councils and individuals that sought to draw people out of the city. Regardless of their origins, our vast number of ocean pools in NSW is testament to the power and lasting benefits of community-led public projects. They provide accessible and equitable infrastructure to a broad cross-section of society, irrespective of their means. The investment made a century ago to build these pools has never been more valued by the community than they are today. This came into sharp focus during the pandemic as ocean pools remained accessible during successive lockdowns while aquatic centres and beaches were closed.

The last ocean pool to be built in Australia was over half a century ago in North Cronulla during the late 1960s. Despite being well loved and iconic, ocean pools are in many ways legacies of another time. They were built long before our current standards of safety, coastal conservation and community expectations. More recently the effects of climate change have become evident and demonstrated that our ocean pools are now vulnerable and in decline. Successive weather systems and bouts of coastal inundation now batter

We live by the sea not simply because it is more pleasant to be a lazy nation, but because of the two mysteries the sea is more forthcoming; its miracles and wonders are occasionally more palpable, however inexplicable they be. There is more bounty, more possibility for us in a vista that moves, rolls, surges, twists, rears up and changes from minute to minute. The innate human feeling from the veranda is that if you look out to sea long enough, something will turn up ...

Tim Winton, *Land's Edge: A Coastal Memoir*

the east coast of Australia with increasing severity and destruction.

This has led us to ask the question: what is the future of our ocean pools and where do they fit in a contemporary sense? To many, the concept of a new ocean pool is a prospect that could never be realized today. Equally, the prospect of losing an existing pool is unanimously opposed by the community. However, there are significant challenges to building and maintaining structures within coastal and intertidal zones. In Australia, development along the coastline is highly regulated and protected because of the value we place on our foreshore as significant public landscapes. Our beaches, rock platforms and headlands underpin coastal ecologies and processes which, if disturbed, can diminish fragile marine life and divert the natural movement of sand and water.

However, the coast is not a static landscape. It is in a constant state of change across vast scales of space and time. More frequently, the impacts of global warming have begun to shape and accelerate these changes. As these impacts take hold, our coastlines are in retreat, pushing back the thin strip of foreshore into the coastal suburbs and cities behind. In Australia and around the world we are seeing harsh defensive seawalls cropping up in an attempt to hold back the tide of change. This has been at odds with communities advocating for conservation of the beach as a natural and publicly accessible landscape. The innate natural beauty of the coast is fiercely defended by communities today.

In an age where we are realizing the importance of environmental stewardship, ocean pools are a masterclass in marrying together the natural and man-made, and designing them to reinforce one another. Rather than a window into the past, they are quickly being recognized as a springboard into the future of coastal architecture and design, paving the way for contemporary and inclusive approaches to inhabiting the coast and reinforcing natural

environmental processes rather than barring them out. Ocean pools afford us an example whereby we can occupy the water's edge while maintaining its natural character and ecological systems. These distinct structures are conspicuously separate from formal aquatic centres, yet they provide greater amenity and access than an open beach. As a typology they suggest our capacity for a much deeper, contemporary and evolving relationship with the coast. They augment and reinforce natural coastal processes and landscapes while allowing these spaces to remain public and accessible.

In recent years, several community groups have seized the opportunity to add to our legacy of ocean pools in Australia. They are also building on this by re-imagining ocean pools in today's terms and within contemporary frameworks. They are using these projects as a vehicle to ask questions and drive outcomes, which benefit their local communities and restore their coastlines. Through this they have challenged how an ocean pool can return the connection our First Nations people have to their coastal lands. They have pursued strategies for inclusive, equitable and dignified access to the coast. They are exploring strategies to support and reinstate natural habitat, ecosystems and processes. They are also establishing a contemporary movement of coastal design, which goes beyond conservation to regenerate and enhance coastal environments.

At the centre of this movement are the questions: what characterizes an ocean pool; why do we value them; and how can this drive future coastal design? These questions, and the significance and preponderance of ocean pools in NSW, are at the heart of my work and body of research titled *The Wild Edge*. Through this project, and for the first time, NSW's 60 ocean pools have been mapped in detail. The research explores what the critical features of an ocean pool are. It also provides guidance for designing this into future structures. Equipped with this research, communities and professionals can draw on this evidence base to drive and inform the restoration of existing pools and proposal of potential new ones.

In the coastal community of Port Macquarie, northern NSW, a group of residents are forerunners in proposing Australia's first ocean pool in 60 years. In collaboration with the residents group, I was commissioned as part of a team to design a new ocean pool for their community. They are also using the project as a vehicle to return a part of the coast to the traditional landowners, the Birpai people. The design for the pool divides the area into zones for different swimming abilities, activities and types of marine life/habitat. Robust concrete walls will enclose the pool to varying degrees and frame iconic views both to and from the pool. The pool is intended to provide inclusive access to the open ocean for the township and its surrounds. Proposed ramps down and into the pool facilitate access for people with varying abilities, from those undergoing rehabilitation to training triathletes and children. Two semi-enclosed, 25m lap lanes offer protection between the children's pool and main lap lanes. These two lanes facilitate buffered swimming conditions, dignified access to the water

for less mobile swimmers and offer guide rails which will assist vision-impaired swimmers. A tapered ramp to the south caters for visitors engaging in active rehabilitation and leisure. A children's swimming area and benched seating nestles into the rock platform and is protected by the seaward-lapping areas from high swell during strong winds. Tucked into the contours of the rock to encourage engagement with the natural landscape, the pool is designed to maintain key vistas of the coast and support intertidal ecosystems.

The proposed pool at Oxley Beach embodies the key characteristics of an ocean pool: to allow swimmers to connect to the coast and ocean, building only where necessary to achieve this. It provides inclusive access to the ocean, supports marine habitats, and acknowledges the role of stewardship the Birpai people play in coastal land management. This shift drives at a contemporary and evolving relationship with the coast in Australia and abroad. It embraces an approach beyond conservation and protection to advocate for ways that we can regenerate the coast, enhancing the natural landscape and ecosystems, and ensuring our continued ability to be coastal dwellers now and well into the future.

Nicole Larkin is an Australian Architect whose practice focuses on Ocean Pool design, planning and conservation. In 2020 Nicole launched The Wild Edge: A Survey of Ocean Pools in NSW *which maps and analyses the Ocean Pools in her home state of NSW. Her work has been widely published and recognized for its contribution to design excellence in the coastal environment.*

COALCLIFF
ROCK POOL

Location Coalcliff, New South Wales
Built 1921–26
Size 27m long
Community Group Stanwell Park Sea Eels
Winter Swimming Club

Coalcliff Rock Pool is sited in a secluded and
peaceful location along the Illawarra coast. In 1796
men stranded from the wrecked ship *Sydney Cove*
noticed exposed coal on the cliffs. They made a fire
from the coal, attracting rescuers – hence the name.
The Coalcliff Mining Company started operations
in 1877, and it was these same miners that brought
explosives and picks to the beach to form the
Coalcliff Rock Pool in the mid-1920s, much like the
miners' pools in Cornwall.

The pool's popularity in the late 1930s led to
various upgrades, resulting in the current twin-pool
arrangement with a small children's pool conjoined
along the landward side. A simple lean-to structure
now provides a place to change but the original
women's changing area used to be a 'space under a
rock overhang, with a hessian curtain rigged up and
"only ladies" splashed in white paint'.

The main pool's seaward edge forms the edge
of the rock plateau into which the pool is cut.
Swimming here at high tide with a swell is
treacherous and there are stories of swimmers being
lifted onto the perimeter wall or effortlessly washed
over. The debate over the relentless battering of
the sea on the coastline, particularly man-made
additions that counter the natural topography, was
brought to a head in 2013 when astonishingly the
local council planned to let ocean pools 'naturally
crumble and wash out to sea'. But a vociferous
campaign led by Coalcliff Community Association
was organized to save the haven, as had happened
previously during a five-year community project
to save the pool in the late 1950s, when the rock
platform had begun to collapse into the sea.

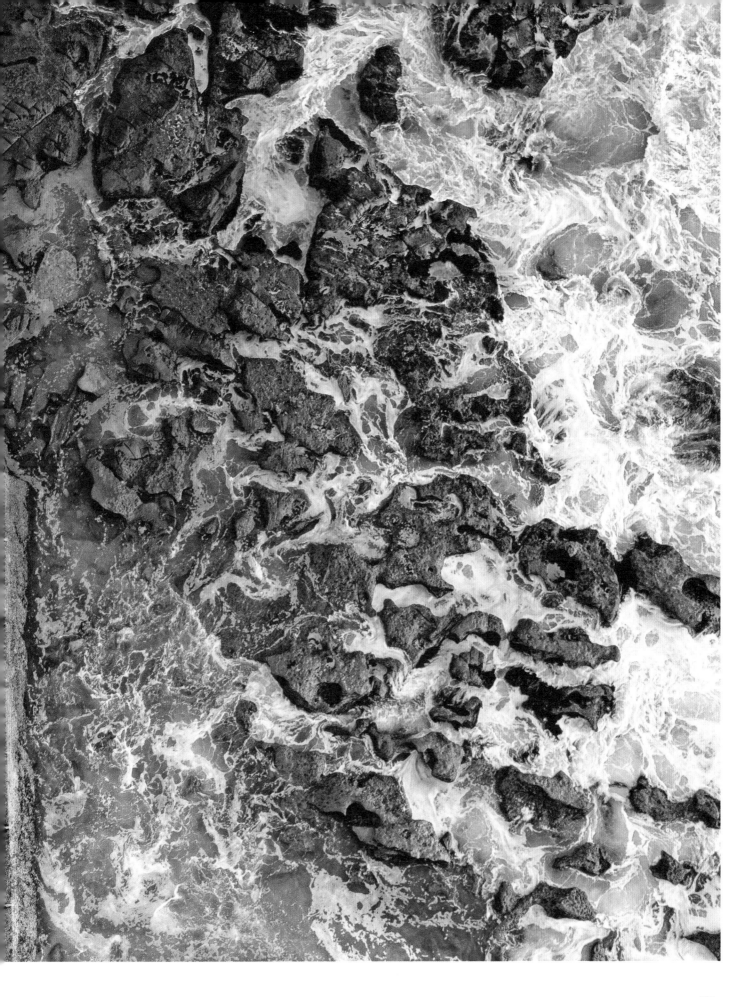

CURL CURL ROCK POOL (NORTH & SOUTH)

Location Curl Curl, New South Wales
Built South 1927; North 1937
Size South 50 x 25m; North 25 x 20m
Community Group Cool Cats Winter Swimming Club; Frigid Frogs Swimming Club; Curl Curl Amateur Swimming Club

These are two contrasting pools positioned at either end of a beach in the northern suburbs of Sydney. The southern pool came first and was funded by the surf club, who raised the money through surf carnivals and social events. The pool opened in 1927 and was extended after just ten years. The wall running down the centre of the current pool marks the outer edge of the original pool. The extended pool formed a secondary area that was deeper and suitable for lengths. In another interesting development, the pool was shortened to 50m in 1966 to enable racing to be undertaken. This created the unique 'stilling basin' to the south-eastern edge. Like its sister pool, the rock plateau pops up in the pool, creating a natural divide between the two pools.

Curl Curl North Rock Pool is believed to be the only NSW ocean pool with a rocky outcrop in its centre. It is rare for a tidal pool to have been built on the north end of a bay, making it vulnerable to heavy seas and swells. However, both obscurities make this a particularly wild place, where the natural elements control who gets access and when. Ten years after it opened, the north pool was destroyed by heavy seas, and it wasn't until around 1957 that it was rebuilt. Nowadays access is only achieved by foot from the headland. The restricted access means the pool is never cleaned; it is at the mercy of nature alone. In 2016 a large boulder the size of a minibus got washed into the pool during a storm, blocking the steps into the water. The pool was closed for an extended time to enable a temporary track to be built and heavy machinery to be brought in to break up the boulder.

EDITHBURGH
TIDAL POOL

Location Edithburgh, South Australia
Built 1880s–1930s
Designer/Engineer Dr Flood
Size 25 x 9.6m
Community Group Edithburgh Swimming Club

Edithburgh is situated on the heel of the Yorke Peninsula in South Australia. By 1900 the town's population had peaked at just over a thousand (it's now around half that figure) and it was the third busiest port in South Australia. The trading prowess of this small town is highlighted by its jetty lying on an axis with the main street. It was at this jetty that locally grown barley and wheat, gypsum and salt were loaded on ships bound for Sydney.

In the 1880s the appropriately named Dr Flood started to form a second tidal pool for Edithburgh. The existing pool to the south side of the jetty was to be reserved for women at a time when mixed bathing was not allowed. The walls of the new pool for men, using local honey-coloured stone and concrete, were not completed before Flood's death. His wife, who had no interest in the project, abandoned the incomplete pool. It wasn't until 1930 that the local corporation and Edithburgh Swimming Club picked up the challenge. The work was painstakingly completed by hand and in 1933 the president of the swimming club, Dick Benbow, opened the pool. When a storm ripped apart the outer wall in 1934, Benbow built it back with a sloping face that withstood the elements for half a century. At the same time, the concrete balcony and terracing was added. Further updates were undertaken in 1983–84 and finally, in 1992, the necessary deepening and lengthening of the pool was funded and opened again by Dick Benbow.

Remarkably the pool has had four names since its inception. Local resident and swimmer Rick Chmielewski notes 'when we chat [about the pool], each person refers to the pool as "my pool"'.

THE GRANT MCBRIDE BATHS

Location The Entrance, New South Wales
Built 50m pool 1938; additional pools 1965
Size Lap pools 50m and 22m long, plus children's pool
Community Group The Entrance Amateur Swimming Club; Tuggerah Tuffs

The Grant McBride Baths, formally known as The Entrance Ocean Baths, is one of only nine ocean pools built on the NSW coast in the 1920s and 30s. In 2002 Member of the State Legislative Assembly for The Entrance, Grant McBride, campaigned with residents to save this important part of the town's social infrastructure from closure. The baths were saved and placed on the NSW Heritage List in 2003. The pool's listing cites their significance because they 'demonstrate the evolution of a simple rock pool known to Aboriginal people as a natural fish trap to a complex of ocean baths'.

The formation of 'Roberts' Pool' in 1919 by Bob Roberts is thought to have evolved out of the Aboriginal fish trap and is noted as one of the more significant sites for linking ocean pools to historic coastal activities. By 1938 the rock plateau that Roberts' Pool was cradled in was buried by the skewed 50m pool. In 1965 the wading pool and 22m pools were plugged in alongside.

The pool is significant as a site that reflects the evolution of coastal recreation in Australia, from secluded bathing to competitive sport. The baths are at the heart of the community and have been since the 1950s when The Entrance Amateur Swimming Club and Entrance Ocean Baths provided free swimming lessons to residents and tourists. Although a pump was added in the 1940s, the pools are still largely filled by the high tide despite their newer, elevated position.

IVO ROWE OCEAN ROCK POOL

Location South Coogee, New South Wales
Built 1920s–30s; altered in 1965
Size 10m wide

Born in 1887, Ivo Rowe was the son of a Cornishman. He lived near the pool and, according to correspondence with his granddaughter, he and his wife were active in the local community. Ivo lived in Coogee until his death. It's unclear what involvement he had in excavating the pool, as records suggest the pool was formed by hand by Giles Darke and his son Sidney Darke in the 1920s and 30s, and then enlarged by Randwick Apex Club in 1965.

This obscure little sister of neighbours Mahon Pool (see pages 146–147) and Wylie's Baths (see pages 158–161) is a shallow and serene pool more suited to a refreshing dip than swimming laps. Intimately connected to the mottled rocks, but set back so you don't have to compete with the ocean swell, the pool used to be referred to as Honeycomb due to the colour and strata of the surrounding rocks.

It's easy to think that one of the smallest pools along the Coastal Walkway might have been formed by potholing. However, closer inspection of this obscure, teardrop pool reveals concrete steps and heavily weathered wooden fence posts to the seaward side of the pool, evidence of human interventions into this plateau.

MAHON POOL

Location Maroubra, New South Wales
Built 1936
Designer/Engineer Alderman Patrick Mahon
Size 30 x 20m
Community Group Maroubra Seals Winter
Swimming Club

Unemployment was rising swiftly during the Great Depression and to bring the situation under control Australian states could apply for government funds to undertake public projects to aid the unemployed in getting back into work. One such Unemployment Relief Scheme was the construction of Mahon Pool. Alderman Patrick Mahon relentlessly lobbied for improvements to this area of Sydney and was the first to present a petition for the pool to Randwick Council. Sadly, Alderman Mahon never saw the finished pool, dying just before its completion.

The suburb of Maroubra is a bustling surfing hotspot, but Mahon Pool is a self-contained retreat from which to explore other delights the sea has to offer – slimy seaweed and local sea life (including lurking sea urchins) share access to the pool. The natural sandstone plateau hosting the pool is surrounded by thriving rockpools teeming with all manner of wildlife that tether the pool to the vast ocean beyond the seaward wall.

The site made use of an existing rockpool and as such less concrete was used in its construction, allowing it to seamlessly nestle in among the rocks, resembling pools found in the North Atlantic. Because of this it is also exposed to the south-westerly winds and can be wild!

MCIVER'S
LADIES BATHS

Location Coogee, New South Wales
Built 1876
Size 34 x 10m
Community Group Randwick & Coogee Ladies
Swimming Association

There are references suggesting that, prior to colonization, the southern end of Coogee Beach was reserved for females and that the site had been a bathing area and birthing place for Aboriginal women. In the 1830s female colonists began swimming at this naturally occurring swimming site. By 1876 the site was officially recognized as a private place for women to bathe.

The pool has long been associated with the rise of women's competitive swimming. In the early 1900s women were forbidden from swimming with men and discouraged from participating in sport. It wasn't until 1912 at the Stockholm Olympics that women were allowed to compete. Swimming for Australia were Fanny Durack and Mina Wylie, who had trained at McIver's and won gold and silver medals respectively.

Protecting the status of the baths as 'the only outdoor ocean swimming venue in continuous use, specifically reserved for women and children in the southern hemisphere' hasn't been easy. In 1946 Randwick Council petitioned the Minister for Lands to approve the baths for mixed bathing. The application was denied. In 1992 a male resident complained to the NSW Anti-Discrimination Board of his exclusion from McIver's, alleging gender discrimination. The case ran for two years before the council unanimously rejected the complainant's case. The council applied for an exemption to the Anti-Discrimination Act, citing the long history of the baths as a space for women and how particular groups of women, including Muslims and refugees, would no longer be able to use McIver's if men were admitted.

I'm delighted this remains a space for those who identify as women. Our cities are richer places for their protected spaces.

MONA VALE POOL

Location Mona Vale, New South Wales
Built 1914
Size 30 x 18 x 0.6–2m
Community Group The Buckettes;
The Bongin Bongin Dawnbusters

Formed from a natural rockpool in the shale rock, the first iteration of this pool opened in 1914 before being enlarged by unemployed labour in the 1930s. The location of the pool is truly magnificent, positioned on a peninsula of rock, with one side partially open to the ocean. A concrete walkway leads back to the sandy beach, yet at high tide the pool becomes encircled in water, floating in the ocean.

The Dawnbusters are a swimming group that sets off from Bongin Bongin Bay every morning, undertaking various distances. There is also the Buckettes, an all-female group founded in 2007. Started by three friends, all over 60, the group has organically grown to 23 members who meet every day at Mona Vale for a swim and coffee. Depending on the surf, it's either into the ocean or pool. The group's name stems from winter swims when the old changing shed had no hot water, according to member Jenny Lewis, quoted in the *Sydney Morning Herald* in 2022: 'Pauline, Margo and I would get so cold that we'd stand in an ice-cream bucket filled with hot water brought from home while we got ourselves dry ... Then, of course, we realized that it was a bit small, so we went out and bought a bigger bucket. And out of that came our name, the Buckettes.'

NEWCASTLE
OCEAN POOLS

Location Newcastle, New South Wales
Built 1819–1935
Designer/Engineer Major Morisset (Bogey Hole);
F.G. Castleden (Newcastle Ocean Baths)
Size Bogey Hole 10 x 6.5 x 1.5m; Newcastle Ocean
Baths 90 x 45m; MOB 100 x 80m
Community Group Merewether Mackerals;
Dixon Park Coldies

Newcastle is blessed with a spectacular history of tidal pools. Stretched out along Bather's Way, the city's coastal path, are five pools built between 1819 and 1935. These pools each provide an insightful history into tidal pool design.

Originally known as the Commandant's Baths, now Bogey Hole Baths, this pool is thought to be the oldest surviving European-built bath in New South Wales. Around 1819, Major James Thomas Morisset instructed a pool to be hewn from the rock plateau for his own personal use. Formed by either convicts or soldiers – the history is unclear – the bath was around 4.5m long, 2m wide and 1.8m deep. It wasn't until 1863 that the bath was entrusted into the hands of the local council for the use of residents. In 1884, due to its popularity, the council increased the size and depth of the pool. The bottom of the pool was said to be 'almost as smooth as a billiard table'. In 1885 a caretaker was introduced, possibly influenced by the British indoor public baths and wash houses. A caretaker's house, changing sheds and spring-fed showers soon followed.

In 1910 the council decided there wasn't an adequate pool for the expanding city. A taxpayer's referendum was held and soon after blasting on a large plateau of rock commenced under the watchful eye of the city engineer. Architect F.G. Castledean was brought in to resolve plans for the buildings and by New Year's Day 1913 the incomplete 'Griffith

Ocean Baths' was opened to huge appreciation. Extra trains were laid on as crowds arrived to witness the varied depth and sparkling clean, European-style seawater baths in operation. Building costs had nearly doubled, though, and when big storms hit, the building work stopped. Castledean was asked to prepare a slimmed-down building proposal and in 1922 the buildings were finally completed.

The success of these baths led to the addition of the adjacent circular children's pool (now called Canoe Pool) and then in 1935, at the southern edge of the city, Merewether Ocean Baths (MOB) opened. Claimed as the largest ocean baths in the southern hemisphere, it sits precariously on the rock plateau like a mirrored tray. The main pool is separated from the children's pool by a wide promenade with benches for watching the swimming. MOB caps off Newcastle's historic tidal pool history with audacious simplicity.

WOONONA
ROCK POOL

Location Woonona, New South Wales
Built 1898; 1929; 1976
Size 50 x 20 x 1.5–2m
Community Group Woonona Ockies

Architect and designer Nicole Larkin describes Collins Rock as 'lots of ghost pools making for an interesting study on iteratively inhabiting the intertidal zone'. She's not wrong. Aerial views of the peninsula are a palimpsest of ocean pools.

The first pool appeared here in 1898. Later, in 1924, an unusual 90m pool began construction under the coordination of the Woonona Surf Club Baths Committee. Volunteers offering their labour were rewarded for their efforts with a keg of beer donated by the Woonona Royal Hotel. Despite the surf club's fundraising efforts, a lack of funds meant the work went on until 1928, and the pool only officially opened in 1929.

The new pool wasn't very successful. Built too close to the sea, it was battered by the ocean and took in a lot of sand. In 1976 the pool currently visible on the site was completed. Woonona Baths Pavilion or Dressing Shed, was a pared-back, Art Deco structure built in concrete by local engineers R.G. Cram & Sons. The design of the pavilion echoed those found in northern Europe, particularly Scotland. A colonnaded front with viewing platform on the roof resembles pavilions from the same era at Saltcoats Bathing Pond (see pages 82–83) and Tarlair Outdoor Pool. Records are vague for the pavilion, but the original structure was demolished in 1994 and rebuilt to the same details on a smaller scale. The turquoise starting blocks suggest that in 1976 competitive swimming was still undertaken at Woonona, when indoor or freshwater pools were far more common.

WYLIE'S BATHS

Location Coogee, New South Wales
Built 1907
Size 46 x 30 x 0.5-1.6m
Community Group Randwick & Coogee Amateur
Swimming Club; Coogee Diggers

How many tidal pools can claim to have been established by a champion long-distance and underwater swimmer, while also being an amateur builder? Just one – Wylie's Baths.

Wylie's is simply one of the finest, if not *the* finest, tidal pool in Australia, possibly the world. As the first mixed-gender baths in Australia, it held the first Australian Swimming Championships and is, according to the Australian National Trust, the oldest surviving communal baths in Australia.

Courtney Tallon, former baths manager, has said, 'If people go to Icebergs [at Bondi Beach] to be seen, then people come to Wylie's to swim with the octopus.'

Wylie's is more than just another pool, it's a place rooted in the cultural history of Australia. Long before Wylie's was built, the site is thought to have held significance for Aboriginal women. When the pool was built in 1907 the venue was closely associated with the development of competitive swimming in Australia. It was Henry Wylie's daughter Mina, and her fierce rival and friend Fanny Durack, who travelled to Sweden for the 1912 Olympic Games. Having overcome stiff opposition in Australia to their participation, Durack achieved gold and Wylie silver in the 100m freestyle.

In both the 1970s and the 1990s Wylie's was closed because of the unsafe condition of the structure. The gnarled, matchstick-thin timber frame and deck that delicately dances across the boulder-strewn cove had entered a precarious state. A major renovation in 1994 was faithful to the original design and invisibly repaired the celebratory pavilions and iconic, mustard-yellow and steel-blue balustrading colours. Despite the weathering this place takes, raising the pavilions way above the pool protected them from the worst of the elements and provided a spacious concrete deck for the community to meet poolside.

YAMBA OCEAN POOL

Location Yamba, New South Wales
Built 1969
Size 30 x 10m

Until 1968 the community of the small seaside
resort of Yamba utilized a disused quarry pit as the
town's swimming pool. Complaints about pollution
at the quarry pool, plus an inspector's confirmation
that the pool was a health hazard, convinced
Maclean Shire Council to build an ocean pool at
Yamba's main surfing beach.

Yamba Ocean Pool opened in 1969. Positioned
on the rock plateau to the southern end of the main
beach, the pool sits perpendicular to the beach. To
the seaward end a short wall encloses a smaller pool
thought to be a stilling basin, like that used at South
Curl Curl Rockpool (see pages 137–139). The short
wall enclosing the basin stretches out across the
plateau, beyond the pool, creating a sheltered area to
sit or enjoy the naturally occurring rockpools.

Yamba is one of the newest pools on the NSW
coastline and yet sits alongside one of the world's
oldest surf lifesaving clubs, founded in 1908,
which uses the pool to train in.

BRONTE BATHS

Location Bronte, New South Wales
Designer/Engineer Alfred Williams
Built 1887
Size 38 x 20m

Despite being reliant on a pump to refresh the water, Bronte Baths is elemental to the history and development of sea bathing.

In 1864, Bronte Park's existence was under threat. To protect it, Sydney's Waverley Council asked the Minister for Lands to place it under the control of the council for public recreation and sea bathing. This is believed to be the first time a municipal council in Australia sought to dedicate an area to sea bathing. 23 years later, an existing bogey hole was enlarged, a sea wall built, and Bronte Baths opened to the public. Supervision for the build was undertaken by Alfred Williams, an engineer with the NSW Dept of Public Works, Harbours and Rivers Branch.

Bronte Baths has been known by various names, including Wylie's Bronte Baths. Harry Wylie took a long lease of the Baths in 1895 during which he offered the latest seawater health cures, presumably inspired by The Royal Sea Bathing Infirmary in Margate, UK amongst other emerging places. Hot sea baths were thought to fix a variety of ailments.

Despite Aboriginal communities having utilized the spaces along the coast for many years prior, the construction of Bondi, Bronte, and other baths along the east coast were permanent markers of a change in attitudes to sea bathing in Australia in line with what was occurring in Europe.

As a result of Bronte Baths success, the community entered the ocean with a newfound confidence in sea bathing. Due to the 'Bronte Express' and other rip currents, vital lifesaving patrols were quickly organised to ensure the safety of fledgling bathers. These Bronte patrols went on to establish surf lifesaving clubs along the coast. There remains much conjecture as to whether Bondi or Bronte had the first club, but Bronte's involvement in this movement is undeniable and the baths hold a special place in the history of ocean baths.

Saltwater sanctuaries

Therese
Spruhan

I lean over the blue and yellow chequerboard deck that stands high above Wylie's Baths, watching waves crash on to the edge and pour white water into the pool. It's almost high tide, and as the sets keep coming the pool overflows, spilling water over the adjoining sandstone like delicate threads of lace. Then there's a break between sets and the water is still for a minute or two. Swimmers in red, blue and yellow caps settle into a rhythm as they lap up and down the pool. Others in snorkels and masks move in circles, their eyes on something they've spotted underneath – sea stars, blackfish or perhaps an octopus hiding in one of the rocky crevices on the natural bottom of the pool.

When the sets start rolling in again, I try to imagine my water-loving mother and her sister at their swimming lessons at the pool 30 years after Henry Wylie excavated it out of the rock platform in 1907. I picture the two freckle-faced girls, enthusiastically following instructions from their teacher, Olympic silver medallist and daughter of Henry, Mina Wylie, strands of their dark-pigtailed hair hanging out of their old-fashioned caps.

My relationship with this sea pool became close in the long winter of 2021. As Covid numbers rose and more and more people became sick, I was grateful to find relief plunging into the saltwater in this magnificent pool at Coogee on the edge of the Sydney coast. I also got a taste for swimming in the colder months and after half an hour of watching silver bream swim across my path and gazing at mother-of-pearl shells, I'd emerge feeling euphoric, like I'd shed a skin and could begin anew again. When I dried off on the concrete beneath the timber deck I'd say: 'Wasn't that sensational?' In between sighs, I'd say it repeatedly to my niece, Mary, who often swam with me, or to my friend Michelle Wheeler, who also discovered Wylie's and winter swimming in lockdown.

'It's magical swimming in a sea pool like Wylie's,' says Michelle, 'but I think you have to go with someone as it's really nice to share how wonderful you feel when you get out.' Michelle likens swimming at Wylie's to an out-of-body experience. 'It sounds a bit crazy, but you don't think about anything except the context that you are in – the beautiful fish you are seeing or that wave that's pounding in and pushing you off course.'

Since that winter, I've returned often to Wylie's, on my own or with Mary or Michelle, and each time I've visited I've noticed something new; something that makes up the character of this pool: the golden banksias that line the steps leading to the striped façade; the sculpture of Mina Wylie, perched above the pool like a sea goddess; Boots, the caretaker's black and white cat, lying in a sunny spot below Mina's feet; and Matthew Martin, the pool's unofficial resident artist, sketching the textures in the sandstone, a bolt in a wooden post, a swimmer mid-stroke.

On the deck after a winter dip, I've rejoiced in the warmth of the sun, and heard stories about the days when Wylie's had a diving tower and slide. I've experienced the calm of low tide and the thrill of standing on the south-west corner when a big swell smashes into the edge, rises and tumbles over me like a waterfall. I've also noticed the small details in and around the pool – the black and white periwinkles and orange seaweed that cling to the edge, and how lovely it is to dive into the water as it ripples out in circles like a kaleidoscope of emerald and blue.

'When you swim in a chlorine pool it's pretty much the same each day,' says Michelle. 'But at Wylie's it's different each time you go because the ocean changes every day. You feel transformed when you get out and I always want to say: "Wow, that was fab!"'

Transformed is a big word, a big concept – making a marked change in form, nature or appearance. But that's exactly what Lai Nguyen says happened to her at McIver's Ladies Baths, a women-only pool just north of Wylie's, built beneath a sandstone cliff in 1876.

'The spirit of McIver's transformed me from a quiet woman of colour to a sociable woman,' says Lai.

She first encountered the pool 10 years ago when a colleague suggested it would help her post-cancer recovery. At that first meeting she couldn't believe the joy she felt standing in the seawater and looking out at the glorious ocean view. The only problem was she couldn't swim. She signed up for lessons at a local aquatic centre but didn't make much progress until she switched to classes at McIver's. With that extra bit of care and individual attention, Lai's technique improved and one day she realized she was swimming.

'At 56 I could finally swim,' she says. 'What a wonderful feeling. The water was holding me up and I was enjoying it; the water was my friend, not my enemy. I was truly transformed in the beautiful seawater of the women's pool.'

Since then, she's become a regular at McIver's. Her transformation has continued, with fellow swimmers helping her with her English pronunciation, something she had struggled with since coming to Australia in 1985 as a refugee from Vietnam.

'These women who are busy volunteering at the pool made time for me, correcting my pronunciation and grammar, and explaining new vocabularies that were easy for me to remember,' says Lai. 'They treated me like one of their dear friends and I was inspired by their kindness. To me they are like the spirit of McIver's Ladies Baths.'

Lynne Spender says the kindness and friendship are not just one-way. 'Lai has become a friend to many and when Covid happened, she made us all masks. She's a wonderful cook, too, and often shares her delicious rice paper rolls with us.'

Friendship is something many people find when they go to sea pools at a similar time each day or through one of the numerous summer and winter swimming clubs – the Maroubra Seals, the Merewether Mackerels, the Bondi Icebergs, to name a few. The community element is what Margi

Gormly loves about swimming at Woonona Rock Pool, a 50m beauty opened in 1929 just south of Sydney on the New South Wales Illawarra coast.

'When you are surrounded by the ocean everyone is happy to have a conversation. All ages come to the pool and people look out for each other,' says Margi, who has been a regular for the past 22 years. She especially remembers the kindness of many of the women who kept watch on her son when he was a baby.

'One woman started it and then others did it too,' says Margi. 'They used to say, "We know what it's like to have a baby. It's no problem; go and do your laps." I'll always remember their kindness and arriving at the pool not feeling great and then diving in and being immediately lifted up.

'And then there are those special days when we spot dolphins swimming with the surfers in the waves, and one time we watched a whale breach in the sea just outside the pool. Everyone got so excited,' Margi says. 'After we wondered if it really happened. Did we really experience something so wonderful?'

That powerful connection with nature keeps drawing me back to sea pools. I vividly remember the chance encounter I had with an eastern blue groper, the chunky ultramarine fish that starts life as a female and turns into a male. I had been about to get out of the water at Giles Baths, an almost natural rock pool at the northern end of Coogee Beach, when all of sudden one appeared in front of me. I spent the next 20 minutes swimming around the pool with him as if I was just another fish. When I got out, I couldn't take the smile off my face.

Artist Lizzie Buckmaster Dove says swimming at her local Coledale sea pool, a presence on the NSW Illawarra coast since 1921, is an essential part of how she maintains connection and balance.

'It's a space, literally for breathing and for finding my breath,' she says. 'And every time I walk across the beach, the rock platform and reach the pool, I'm wowed by its existence, its elemental nature, its liminal qualities, in between the land and the sea.'

I have similar feelings of excitement when I meet a sea pool for the first time. A vivid memory is spotting the Art Deco pavilion of Newcastle's ocean baths, dating from around 1922, as I walked along the seafront. I'd read that the early designers had envisaged the pool being artistic and substantial and that's exactly what I found. The façade of the cream-coloured pavilion was decorated with diamond shapes and lines of colour in pink, purple, yellow and turquoise. When I walked through the entrance, I found an enormous pool separated into two by a timber walkway, and a huge concrete wall on the northern side with levelled seating where bodies lay in the sun.

The Newcastle Ocean Baths have been a favourite subject for artist James Willebrant; he started painting them in the early 1970s in his distinctive surrealist mixed with pop-art style. He says he's drawn to the beauty and faded glory of the Art Deco style and the structures in and around the pool.

'I love the sweeping perspectives, the angles, the whitewashed concrete starting blocks, and the wonderful stepped turquoise wall that's so distinctive to the baths, with its curve at one end,' says James. 'The pool is very nostalgic for me, and I have a real affection for it because I've known it for such a long time. I've used it physically to swim in and imaginatively in my paintings. I think it will always be with me in my work.'

Sea pools affect us, and they have the capacity to give us what we need: inspiration, a break from the world, a dose of saltwater, beauty – even love.

That's what Colleen Kelly found when she wagged school aged 12 and wandered into McIver's Ladies Baths, the same pool where Lai Nguyen's life was transformed. Inside she met a woman she calls Mrs C, who made space for her on the bench, gave her cake, wrapped her in a towel and rubbed her back.

'It was the first time I'd experienced love,' says Colleen, who grew up in children's homes. After that day, she went back each week until one night she was moved to another home far away from Coogee.

But she never forgot Mrs C and the pool. When she retired, she reconnected by becoming a volunteer and a regular swimmer there. She says Mrs C saved her life and that memory of her helped her many times during difficult periods. And now when she swims in the pool, she says it always gives her a hug.

'It holds me, and I feel that lovely, gentle rocking motion and it takes me back to my original meeting with Mrs C and our beloved women's pool.'

On 21 June, I return to Wylie's just before sunrise for the winter solstice. Above the pool where my mother and aunty swam, the sky is resplendent in pink, purple and navy blue. Then it becomes a mix of apricot, watermelon and finally a brilliant orange and yellow. When I dive in, the colours of the sunrise reflect in the water, and I feel like I've been transported to paradise. Groups of friends hold hands and leap in, others drift around the water and float. 'Beautiful,' I say over and over again as gentle waves wash in pouring champagne bubbles over my head.

Therese is a Sydney swimmer, writer and author. In 2019, her first book, The Memory Pool: Australian Stories of Summer, Sun and Swimming *was published by NewSouth, and in 2021, her writing was featured in* The Women's Pool. *She writes about pools on her blog,* Swimming Pool Stories *and posts photos on Instagram @swimmingpoolstories.*

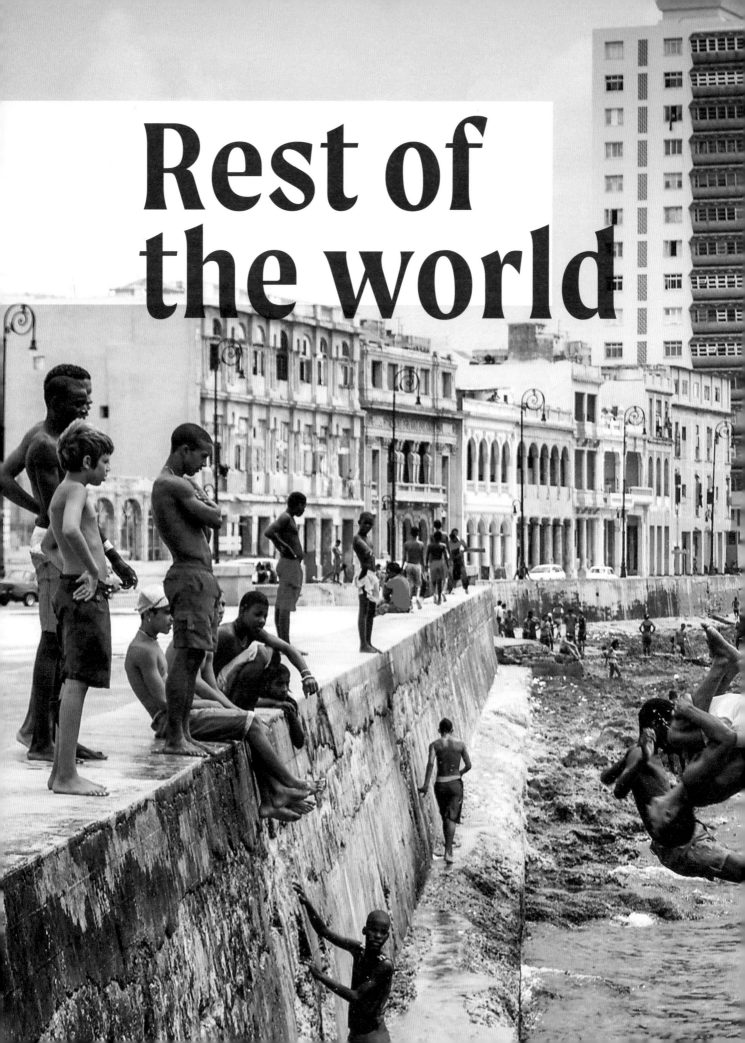

Rest of the world

ALI'I SALTWATER POOL

Location Kona, Big Island, Hawaii, USA
Size 20 x 15m

Huge Pacific Ocean waves crash against the face of this curvaceous pool. Swimmers sat or standing on the outer wall are swept into the surf as the rollers crash into the foreshore. The pool water is calm, and so it is a popular destination for families and, facing west in among the palm trees, provides a perfect spot for sunsets.

Positioned on top of the rocky foreshore, the pool is like a decapitated volcano. The basin is formed in concrete, but the outer faces are wrapped in a sloping stone. This pool, which was formerly privately owned but is now publicly accessible, has been disguised to sit harmoniously within the geology of the area.

BAÑOS DE MAR

Location Malecón, Havana, Cuba
Built From 1864

Malecón de La Habana was originally conceived by US authorities at the end of the nineteenth century to accommodate the growing city of Havana. Work didn't commence until 1900, at which point it began to build over a stretch of rocky and inhospitable coastline that had several *baños de mar* (sea bathing stations) located along it. Although Cuba has spectacular sandy beaches, not everyone could get to them and the *baños* offered free and safe bathing for lower-income families.

The pools were often dynamited out of the rock and varied in size, mostly around 2m square and 1–2m deep. Each had steps cut into the rock to access the pool, and a couple of openings through which seawater flowed in and out, ensuring a reasonably fresh supply of water. The bottom was often covered in sand and shells, giving it a white, beach-like appearance. They were built at public expense and the basic pools were free to use, although they were divided by gender and skin colour. The pool was covered with a timber roof or awnings and the sides were also screened to guarantee privacy.

One of the most famous was Palacio de Carneado. Unlike some of the more upmarket *baños*, they didn't offer orchestras and brass bands for the obligatory dance after a swim. In fact, the owner of Palacio de Carneado, José Carneado, was probably more famous for his eccentricities. Carneado boasted that its waters were the clearest and healthiest on the coast and insisted that the absence of dance floors gave tranquillity and calm to customers with 'their spirits low'. The Cuba-loving Spaniard was inclined to boast about his wealth, his physical strength and his manhood. Indeed, placed on the outside of his house was a statue of himself, appearing naked with muscles in tension, overlooking the ocean.

Today the *baños* are buried under the Malecón with just a few of the man-made pools still visible and used by children. The water quality is poor, and the sea can become very rough, but the kids and young men swim here regardless.

LA CARPA OLIVERA

Location Mazatlán, Sinaloa, Mexico
Built 1914
Designer/Engineer Antonio Olivera
Size 19 x 16 x 1.4m

When chef Antonio Olivera arrived by boat in Mazatlán in the 1910s, his vision was for a pool and restaurant inspired by the pier structures in his home city of Lisbon and the Portuguese coast. Despite opening his new business when the Mexican Revolution was entering Sinaloa (or perhaps because of it), the place was a huge success. The Mexican glitterati and families flocked to the pool, restaurant and bar.

If all tidal pools were graced with a slide as exuberant as this one, surely we could banish all indoor verruca-ridden leisure centres? The corkscrew slide is a later addition by architect Erick Pérez with Colectivo Urbano. The architects' collective restored the pool in 2014 after a series of devastating hurricanes smashed into the coastline between 1957 and 1975. It is now managed by the municipality but remains a social hub for the community.

HEPING ISLAND POOL

Location Heping Island Park, Keelung, Taiwan
Built 1981/1985
Size Blue Ocean 50 x 25 x 2.5m; pet pool
25 x 15 x 2.5m

Until the 1970s, Keelung was a military playground, largely concealing the spectacular zoomorphic sandstone coastline sculpted by years of erosion.

Tucked away on the western flank of this strategic island is an expansive concrete terrain. Reminiscent of a lorry park, or failed theme park, the neo-Spanish seventeenth-century fort, sand pits and, finally, undulating cobbled forms lead to three heroic tidal pools. The scale of this facility is extraordinary, particularly compared to its discreet sibling, Keelung Haixing Swimming Association pool.

This is an astonishing place with a complex background. As with Haixing, the history is wrapped up in a booming aquaculture. Tales of both legal and illegal abalone farming crop up in most stories. It's pure conjecture, but the largest pool, called the Blue Ocean Pool, may have been built by the military before being converted for abalone farming. It wasn't until 1985, when the natural beauty of the area was formally recognized, that Heping Island Park was established and the pools were turned to recreational use.

The Blue Ocean Pool is split into two, with a smaller pool to the west with bridge access. Signs indicate that pets are permitted into this pool, subject to wearing a lifejacket! The larger section has two lanes marked on the base. Two, because the pool curiously has two piers jutting out into the pool that create a pinch point, limiting the swimmable area. The seawall is at least 4m wide with two flared openings for the sluice gates. Perimeter walls are accompanied by inner walls, creating channels that appear to have no legitimate use within a swimming pool. These are most likely left over from aquaculture or military use. To the east is the wading pool, bordered by a high-level concrete walkway that leads from the neo-Spanish fort pavilion. The final pool is nestled in the sandstone and looks like an adapted natural rockpool.

KAMOGAURA
SALTWATER POOL

Location Wajima, Ishikawa, Japan
Built From 1935
Size 25 x 13m

Kamogaura is at the northernmost tip of a peninsula near Wajima on the Sea of Japan. The area is intensely beautiful with a coastline populated by reefs.

This saltwater pool was built because, in the early Showa period (the reign of Emperor Hirohito), there were no school pools and children used to swim in the sea. The local swimming association instigated a campaign to build a pool and started collecting donations; from around 1935 building work was able to start on an outdoor pool cut from the rocky coastline. The Second World War delayed the completion of the pool but by 1949 it was ready. In 1950 the concrete surrounds were added, along with the numbered lanes visible at either end.

Seawater naturally flows in and out of from the north and south intakes. Tidal pools are rare in Japan, so the facility has become an asset for the community. Olympic silver medal winners Tsuyoshi Yamanaka (Melbourne 1956 and Rome 1960) and Yoshihiko Osaki (Rome 1960) both trained in the pool.

KEELUNG HAIXING SWIMMING ASSOCIATION

Location Keelung, Taiwan
Size 20 x 15m

The backdrop is raw and industrial but there is something special about this pool. Run by the elusive Keelung Haixing Swimming Association, there is a longer history to this pool yet to be unravelled.

The swimming is split into three areas. A pentagon-shaped tidal pool around 1.2m deep is separated from a sheltered area between the rocky shoreline. Beyond that is open sea. Large reefs cause steep drop-offs in depth, but the concrete platforms continue to entice the youth to venture beyond the shelter of the pool. Despite its ramshackle appearance, lifeguards are on patrol during holidays and many locals learn to swim alongside the flourishing wildlife in this free-to-access pool. It appears to be something of a local secret.

Rock armour is prevalent on three sides of the tidal pool, which is reminiscent of the heavy weave used for a winter blanket. Somehow a steel-mesh platform sits within this weave and distinctly Heath Robinson showers are provided within the complex geometric landscape.

Despite the blue steel stairs having seemingly been dropped in without much thought to their appearance, they are in fact delicate and striking. Along with the linear platform above, the flimsiness of the structure is fabulous against the concrete rock armour.

LAGUNA BEACH POOLS

Location South Laguna Beach, California, USA
Size William E. Brown's pool 13 x 15m

The city of Laguna Beach has an 11km coastline. Along it, crumbling and undulating sandstone cliffs give way to a total of 27 sandy beaches and coves. By the late nineteenth century Laguna Beach was a recognized tourist attraction despite the area only having around 300 residents. Its proximity to Hollywood attracted visitors from the creative industries and private houses precariously jostle for position along the cliff's edge.

Midway along the Laguna Beach coastline is Victoria Beach. In 1926 William E. Brown, a senator from LA, built an 18m Romanesque tower to enclose a stairway down to the beach. At its base, Brown also built a D-shaped concrete pool, the remains of which are gradually being consumed by the sand. The landward side has now all but disappeared and the pool appears an elegant horseshoe shape. It once sat about 1.5m above the beach with direct access to a stair back to the clifftop house. At high tide the pool's brow takes the force of the incoming waves, throwing spray over swimmers. At low tide the water flows away, leaving a medallion of dry sand.

Further south from Victoria Beach, at the end of North La Senda Drive, is a small cove. Here there is a rectangular pool and at least another five irregular ones set within the intertidal zone at the base of the cliff face. As with the Victoria Beach pool, these were built by owners of the properties above and accessed via a staircase down the face of the cliff. The largest of the five, the Edward Griffith Pool, is approached via a concrete bridge from the base of a private stair. About 20m long, the pool has a broad walkway around the edge. The seaward corner has been nibbled by the sea but otherwise the structure remains in good shape and is used by those that can find a way to it. Further south, a second pool is a more organic shape, presumably to follow the natural formation of the rock plateau.

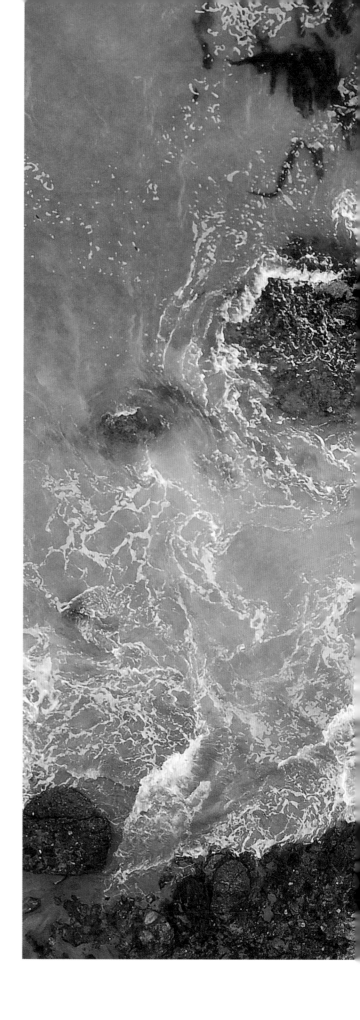

FURTHER READING

Bezuidenhout, Vincent, 'Separate Amenities' (essay, 2011)

Deakin, Roger, *Waterlog* (Chatto & Windus/Vintage, 1999)

Frampton, Kenneth, *Álvaro Siza Vieira: A Pool in the Sea* (Actar Publishers, 2018)

Jones, Lucy, *Losing Eden* (Penguin, 2010)

Love, Christopher (Ed.), *A Social History of Swimming in England 1800–1918* (Routledge, 2008)

Mac Evilly, Brendan, *At Swim* (The Collins Press, 2015)

McDermott, Marie-Louise, 'Wet, Wild & Convivial' (thesis, 2012)

Parr, Susie, *The Story of Swimming* (Dewi Lewis Media, 2011)

Pusill, Emma and Wilkinson, Janet, *The Lido Guide* (Unbound, 2019)

Spender, Lynne (Ed.), *The Women's Pool* (Spinifex 2021)

Spruhan, Therese, *The Memory Pool* (NewSouth Publishing, 2019)

Worpole, Ken, *Here Comes the Sun* (Reaktion Books, 2000)

PICTURE CREDITS

Chris is co-founder of architects Studio Octopi where he leads on all the watery projects in the practice. His work on improving access to water for all is central to the Future Lidos Group that he helped establish in 2023. When he's not immersed in water, he's juggling other passions such as London Modern, a modernism festival for London.
@sea.pools @chrisromerlee

ACKNOWLEDGMENTS

For Dad and his love of the sea

This book wouldn't have been possible without the unfaltering love and support of my parents, Diana and Daniel. Huge thanks must go to my wife, Alex, who believed in me and threw me numerous lifelines. Special mention to my long-suffering tidal poolers, Orson and Juno, Beany and Paul who pointed me to Granville, and my brother-in-law James Bollen in Taiwan.

Leo Hollis for awakening me to what I was about to undertake and my business partner James Lowe for tolerating me. Arduous research trips to Ireland with Simon Warren (450 miles in three day) and France with Phil Luther and Ben Wyatt (300 miles in three days) thankfully didn't dent 40-year friendships. My Serpentine swim buddy Peter Morris propelled me on through the seasons.

Gathering the material for the book I relied on enthusiastic and generous people the world over. In Australia, I couldn't have done it without Nicole Larkin and Therese Spruhan's knowledge and contacts, particularly Marie-Louise McDermott, Courtney Tallon and Rick Chmielewski.

In South Africa, thanks go to Kevin Fellingham, Lisa Beasley, Andre Malan, Anthony Wain, Mary McKenzie, OvP and GAPP Architects and everyone at the City of Cape Town who helped. Langstrand in Namibia was the toughest pool to crack and eventually all roads led to Eddie Bosman. Thank you to the people of Langstrand, Tourism Walvis Bay, Yvette Loots and Marli Geldenhuys.

In the UK, sharing databases and tidal pool definitions with Freya Bromley and Jo Halstead expanded my thinking. My thanks to Ruth and Fran Pender, Zoe Latham, Chris Smith, Carole Green and Karin Easton of Perranzabuloe Museum, Rob Newquay, Robin Tapp and the owners of Lewinnick Cove House. Dr Karen Shepherdon, Kathryn Ferguson, in Kent and in the Isle of Man, Sandra Badcock, Charles Guard, Mark Gorry and Dr Breesha Maddrell. In Scotland, the communities caring for The Trinkie and North Baths, Stewart McGookin and Duncan Ford, Ranger for Hoddom and Kinmount Estates.

There are many others who've gone the extra mile, in particular Alex Mira, Michelle Healy, Barbara Harding, Roberto Medeiros, Anais Carpenter, Javier Hidalgo Tugores, Ivan Power, Javier Galindo, Katie Chuang of Heping Island Park, and Johanna Ellis of Laguna Beach Historical Society.

I couldn't have done this without the support of everyone at Batsford including Gemma, Frida, Polly and of course the unflappable patience of my editor Lilly Phelan.

Finally, all the pools that didn't make the cut, there's always the next gala.

INDEX